JN418576

Grammar for Writing in English

CONTENTS

Fun English !!
Apples
Bee
Crown

Unit 1 Present Tense: Simple vs. Present Continuous

Test yourself!

Complete each sentence with proper words and expressions.

(1) A: ______________________________?

B: Yes, I want to eat spaghetti for dinner.

(2) A: Does he enjoy horror movies?

B: No, ____________________.

(3) A: ________________________?

B: The train leaves at 9 pm.

(4) Mary's children love to play soccer in the park. Mary usually takes them to the park. Today, however, they ____________________ because Mary has to go to the doctor's office.

(5) A: ______________________________?

B: I am not quite satisfied with the results because the judge seems unfair.

Grammar Tips!

영어에서 불변의 진리, 지속되거나 규칙적으로 일어나는 행동이나 사건, 일반적인 사실을 이야기할 때 단순 현재 시제 (present simple tense)를 사용한다. 이때 주의할 것은 주어가 3인칭 단수일 경우 (he, she, it, Mary, the girl) 동사의 뒤에 -(e)s를 붙여야 한다. (Subject-Verb Agreement Rule: 주어-동사 수의 일치)

A. Present Simple Tense

The Han River flows across Seoul dividing the south side and north side of Seoul.

They live in New York with two dogs and one cat.

These two sentences describe the current status of the subjects (e.g. flowing across Seoul, living in New York) using the 'Present Simple Tense'. Do you notice the different forms of the verbs? The river flows and they live.

If you say, the river flow and they lives, they are not correct because they violate Subject-Verb Agreement rule. In other words, you need to be careful to add an -(e)s to the verb when a 3rd person singular noun (Mary, Mr. Black) or pronoun (she/he/it) is a subject in a sentence.

1. How to make affirmative statements using the present simple tense

S (I/you/they) + V	S (he/she/it) + V −(e)s
go ➲ go, work ➲ work	go ➲ goes, work ➲ works
(a) I go to school every Wednesday. (b) They work late at night. (c) You are still pretty.	(d) He goes shopping on weekends. (e) Mr. Smith works for the bank. (f) She is interested in pop music.

2. How to make negative statements using the present simple tense

S (I/you/they) + do not + V S + am/are + not	S (he/she/it) + does not + V S + is + not
(a) Most children like ice cream. ➲ Most children do not (=don't) like ice cream. (b) You are scared. ➲ You are not scared. (c) I often attend the meetings. ➲ I do not (=don't) often attend the meetings.	(d) She is smart. ➲ She is not (=isn't) smart. (e) He studies Spanish. ➲ He does not (=doesn't) study Spanish. (f) The baby cries all the time. ➲ The baby doesn't cry all the time.

3. How to make questions using the present simple tense

Do + S (I/you/they) + V? Am/Are + S?	Does + S (she/he/it) + V? Is + S?
(a) They like to go hiking. ➲ **Do they like** to go hiking? Yes, they do. / No, they don't. (b) **Am I** too fast? Yes, you are. / No, you aren't. (c) Where **do you want** to have dinner? I want to eat at Garcia's.	(d) She is satisfied with the result. ➲ **Is she** satisfied with the result? Yes, she is. / No, she isn't. (e) Why **does he want** to come here? He wants to come here because he feels lonely.

Practice 1) Unscramble the given words in a correct order. If the sentence is a question, put a question mark at the end.

1. ______________________________

(sophomore, in, major, I'm, information sociology, a, and)

2. ______________________________

(often, he, himself, to, does, the, go, park, by)

3. ______________________________

(cook, eat, have, to, whenever, like, don't, time, out, they, to, they)

4. ______________________________

(with, she, parents, live, does, her)

5. ______________________________

(off, the, when, out, please, in, go, turn, lights, room, the, you, all)

B. Present Continuous Tense

1. Present continuous tense describes what is happening right now!

(a) I eat instant noodles for lunch.	Present simple tense
(b) I am eating instant noodles for lunch.	Present continuous tense

In case of sentence (a) 'I eat instant noodles for lunch', it means instant noodles are a regular lunch menu for the person. In sentence (b) 'I am eating instant noodles', however, it only indicates that the person is eating instant noodles now, but it does not give any information about lunch for yesterday or tomorrow. To describe something that is happening now but not permanently or regularly, we use 'be + ~ing' form, and it is called 'Present Continuous Tense' in English.

2. Present continuous tense describes what is happening around the moment of speaking.

(c) I am busy these days. I am preparing for the entrance exam and also working at the café in the evenings.
(d) Jim lives with his parents, but this week he is staying with his friends to finish the project.

In sentences (c) and (d), present continuous tense describes what's happening about the time the speaker is talking, not exactly at the moment of talking.

3. Present continuous tense describes one action that is in progress when another action takes place or two actions are taking place at the same time.

(e) He is often sleeping when his friend visits him.
(f) Jane is watching TV while Tom is doing his homework.

Sentence (e) shows that when the second action (visit from a friend) happens, the first action (his sleeping) is in progress. Also, as in (f), present continuous tense can express two different actions in progress at the same time.

4. How to make affirmative statements using present continuous tense

S + be (am/is/are) + ~ing (present participle: 현재분사)
He is usually playing a video game when his mother calls him. They are planning to move to New York. You are eating ice cream too much lately.

5. How to make negative statements using present continuous tense

S + be (am/is/are) + not + ~ing
I am not going to his party now. Mr. Wilson and Ms. Wong are not (= aren't) seeing each other these days. The research team is not (= isn't) making much progress.

6. How to make questions using present continuous tense

Be (Am/Is/Are) + S + ~ing?
Am I talking too fast? Are the students preparing for the exam? Is the new tool increasing the productivity of this unit?

In present continuous tense, 'be' verb functions as a modal in negative statements or questions. Also, '~ing' form in present continuous is present participle (현재분사), not a gerund (동명사).

7. Stative (non-action) Verbs in Present Tense

To make present continuous tense, the verb needs to express any type of action. However, there are some verbs in English that describe conditions or situations that exist. These verbs are called stative verb (상태동사). You cannot use present continuous tense with these verbs.

(a) The spaghetti tastes great. (O)
(b) The spaghetti is tasting great. (X)
(c) The cook is tasting the spaghetti. (O)*

(d) I believe he will succeed in the future. (O)
(e) I am believing that he will succeed in the future. (X)

(f) I don't know him well. (O)
(g) I am not knowing him well. (X)

As you see in the example, when the verb 'taste' describes the state of the subject (~한 맛이 나다), you can't use continuous tense as in (b). However, in sentence (c)*, the verb 'taste' (음식의 맛을 보다) is describing an action that the cook is doing, i.e., tasting the spaghetti. In this case, present continuous tense can be used. On the other hand, verbs like 'believe' and 'know' only have stative meanings as in (d) and (f). In this case, you cannot use present continuous tense with these verbs like in (e) and (g).

Grammar Tips!

영어에서 상태를 나타내는 non-actions verbs (know, believe)는 현재 진행형을 사용할 수 없는데, 그 이유는 상태동사는 행동의 변화를 나타낼 수 없기 때문이다. 예를 들어 한국어에서 '난 요즘 그 사람에 대해 점점 알아가는 중이야' 라로 말한다면 이것을 영어로 고쳤을 때 I am knowing him more and more these days. (X) 라고 할 수 없는데 이는 know라는 동사는 영어에서 진행을 쓸 수 없는 상태동사이기 때문이다. 이런 경우 I am getting to know him more and more these days. (O) 혹은 I am learning more about him these days. (O) 라는 식으로 get to know 라는 형태를 만들어서 get (-되어지다) 의 진행형을 만들든지 아니면 learn 이라는 동사를 사용해서 진행형을 표현할 수 있다.

Common verbs that have stative meanings

Mental state	know realize understand recognize	believe feel suppose think*	imagine* doubt* remember* forget*	want* need desire mean*
Emotional state	love like appreciate please prefer	hate dislike fear envy	mind care	astonish amaze surprise
Possession	possess	have*	own	belong
Sense perception	taste* smell*	hear feel*	see*	
Other existing states	seem look* appear* sound resemble look like	cost* owe weigh* equal	be* exist matter	consist of contain include*

(The verbs with * on the list are ones that can be used as both non-action (stative) and action verbs.

Practice 2) Correct the errors in each sentence. Each sentence has one error.

1. I'm not knowing Sam's wife.

   ☞ Correction:

2. Right now, Tom studying English for the exam.

   ☞ Correction:

3. Do they watching the baseball game?

   ☞ Correction:

4. The soup tastes too sweet. I am not liking it.

   ☞ Correction:

5. This class is consisting of twenty five students from all over the world.

   ☞ Correction:

8. Other usage of present continuous tense

(a) Mary is arriving in Tokyo tomorrow.
  = Mary **will arrive** in Tokyo tomorrow.
(b) Are you meeting him this Saturday?
  = **Will** you **meet** him this Saturday?

(c) Mary **is** very quiet.
(d) Tom **is being** very quiet today. Is he sick?
(e) Sally **is not being** responsible these days. I need to talk to her.
(f) Ms. Kim is being old. (X)

As in sentences (a) and (b), present continuous tense can also describe something that will take place in the near future. In this case, you can replace be ~ing with will + verb to express the future tense.

In addition, sometimes 'be + an adjective' is used in the progressive form of 'be + being + an adjective' when it describes temporary behavior. For example, sentence (c) describes Mary's character (quiet), while in (d) Tom is usually not very quiet, but he is now very quiet for a short duration of time. Likewise, the sentence (e) indicates that Sally is usually very responsible person, but she is not responsible these days temporarily.

Grammar Tips!

be + adjective (형용사)는 일반적인 성향 기질을 표현하는 것에 반하여 be + being + 형용사를 쓰는 것은 최근에 (주로 일시적으로 일어나는) 성향, 상태의 변화를 표현하는 유용한 어구이다. 예를 들어, He is silly. 라고 하면 (그는 바보같아, 멍청해) 라는 뜻으로 그 사람의 전반적인 성향 및 성질을 표현하지만, He is being silly these days after meeting her. (그가 그 여자를 만난 이후로는 요즘 좀 멍청해 진 것 같아.) 라는 뜻으로, 원래 그렇지 않은데 요즘 좀 그렇다는 상태의 변화를 표현한다. 하지만 상태 변화를 표현하는 'be being + adj (형용사)' 어구를 만들 수 없는 형용사들이 있는데 그 예로는 다음과 같다: angry, beautiful, handsome, happy, healthy, hungry, lucky, nervous, sick, tall, thirsty, young.

Practice 3) Complete each sentence using the given word(s).

1. A: Close your eyes. Now listen carefully. What (I, do)____________________?
   B: I think you (rub) ____________________ your hands together now.

2. My mom (look) ____________________ out the window now. It (look) ________ very windy.

3. John (have) ____________________ a very expensive car. However, because of the car, he (have) ____________________ a hard time paying off his debt.

4. I (think) ____________________ my major is not for me, so I (think) ____________________ about changing my major these days.

5. He is a very strict man. However, he (be) ____________________ generous these days probably because he likes the woman in the HR Department.

Practice 4) Translate the following sentences into English using clue words given in parentheses.

1. 난 그 반지 살 여유가 없어. 이건 너무 비싸.
   (ring, afford, cost)

2. 난 그 사람의 행동을 용납할 수 없어요. 요즘 너무 기분 나쁘게 굴어요.
   (approve of, behavior, unpleasant)

3. Jack과 Jill이 요즘 사귀고 있어. 주말마다 함께 나가는 걸.
   (see each other, go out)

4. Tom의 부모님은 그가 회사에서 돌아오는 대로 런던으로 떠나신대요.
   (as soon as, leave for)

Unit in a Nutshell

- In describing something that is true all the time or happens regularly or habitually, use simple present tense.
- When the subject is 3rd person singular noun or pronoun, add -(e)s to the verb.
- In describing something that is happening at the moment, for a short duration of time, or in the near future, use present continuous tense.
- With non-action verbs, don't use present continuous tense.

Practice 5) Correct or Incorrect?

Read the following sentences. If the sentence is correct, circle C. If it is not correct, circle IC. If you circle IC, correct the mistakes.

1. He works too much. I think he is needing some rest now. (C IC)

   ☞ Correction:

2. I am not feeling well today. Can I cancel the meeting in the afternoon?

   (C IC)

   ☞ Correction:

3. Tom is being nervous as his turn is approaching in the competition.

   (C IC)

   ☞ Correction:

4. I am appreciating very much all your care and time. (C   IC)

☞ Correction:

5. Judy is sending her cat to her grandmother tomorrow because she leave town. (C   IC)

☞ Correction:

Writing in Action

Task1.

Traveler's Moment: Describing the picture

Look at the pictures below and write a paragraph to describe each picture. When you write, imagine you are travelling to these places and taking these pictures by yourself. To make the scenes alive, use present simple tense or present continuous tense in your writing.

To generate ideas for the writing, first ask yourself the following questions.

(1) Where is it and who is in the picture?

(2) What are they doing? Or what is happening?

(3) What are they wearing? How do they look?

(4) What's the overall atmosphere of the place in the picture?

Unit 1 Answer Key

Test yourself! (p. 5)

(1) A: Do you want to eat spaghetti for dinner?

B: Yes, I want to eat spaghetti for dinner.

(2) A: Does he enjoy horror movies?

B: No, he doesn't.

(3) A: When does the train leave?

B: The train leaves at 9 pm.

(4) Mary's children love to play soccer in the park. Mary usually takes them to the park. Today, however, they are not going to the park because Mary has to go to the doctor's office.

(5) A: Why aren't you satisfied with the results?

B: I am not quite satisfied with the results because the judge seems unfair.

Practice 1) (p. 8)

1. I'm a sophomore and major in information sociology.
2. Does he often go to the park by himself?
3. They like to eat out whenever they don't have time to cook.
4. Does she live with her parents?
5. When you go out, please turn off all the lights in the room.

Practice 2) (p. 13)

1. I do not know Sam's wife.
2. Right now, Tom is studying English for the exam.

3. Are they watching the baseball game?
4. The soup tastes too sweet. I don't like it.
5. This class consists of twenty five students from all over the world.

Practice 3) (p. 14)

1. A: Close your eyes. Now listen carefully. What am I doing?
   B: I think you are rubbing your hands together now.
2. My mom is looking out the window now. It looks very windy.
3. John has a very expensive car. However, because of the car, he is having a hard time paying off his debt.
4. I think my major is not for me, so I am thinking about changing my major these days.
5. He is a very strict man. However, he is being generous these days probably because he likes the woman in the HR Department.

Practice 4) (p. 15)

1. I can't afford the ring. It costs too much.
2. I don't approve of his behavior. He is being unpleasant these days.
3. Jack and Jill are seeing each other. They go out together every weekend.
4. Tom's parents are leaving for London as soon as Tom returns from work.

Practice 5) (p. 16)

1. IC : is needing → needs
2. C
3. IC : being nervous → nervous
4. IC : am appreciating → appreciate
5. IC : leave → is leaving

Unit 2 Simple Past vs. Present Perfect

Test yourself!

Complete each sentence with proper words and expressions.

(1) A: ______________________________?

B: I went there with my friend Jeff.

(2) A: Did she like moving to the new school?

B: No, ____________________.

(3) John's mother believed that John went to hospital after school. However, it was not true. John ____________________________.

(4) They carry a lot of boxes every day, but ____________________ boxes yesterday due to heavy rain.

(5) A: Did he go to the party or to the library last night?

B: Well, __________________________. He had to study for the final exam.

Grammar Tips!

영어에서 일반동사가 쓰인 문장의 의문문이나 부정문을 만들 때 do 조동사 (do/does)를 사용하는데, 시제가 과거인 경우는 do/does 대신 과거형 did 를 사용한다. 문장에서 do 조동사를 쓸 경우, 본동사는 시제에 상관없이 항상 원형을 써야 한다는 것에 주의! (예: He loved to eat out, but she **did not like** to eat out.)

A. Simple Past Tense

> I **went** to Jeju Island with my friends two years ago.
>
> He already **watched** the movie in the U.S. before it was released in the cinema.

These two sentences simply describe what happened in the past (e.g. going to Jeju Island, watching a movie). In explaining actions or events in the past, the verb form is changed (e.g. work ➡ worked), and this tense is called **Simple Past Tense**.

1. How to make affirmative statements using simple past tense

Regular verbs (add –d/–ed to a base form)	Irregular verbs (Memorize!)
watch ➡ watch**ed**, cook ➡ cook**ed**	come ➡ **came**, go ➡ **went**, am ➡ **was**
(a) Mr. Brown cooked a delicious dinner for his friends.	(b) He went away to hear the news.

2. How to make negative statements using simple past tense

S + did not + base form	S + be + not
(a) He came home. ➡ He did not come home. (b) She cooked the meal. ➡ She did not cook the meal.	(c) She was smart. ➡ She was not smart. (d) They were together then. ➡ They were not together then.

3. How to make questions using simple past tense

Did + S + base form?	Be + S?
(a) I watched TV. ➡ Did you watch TV? Yes, I did. / No, I didn't. (b) Where did she eat dinner? She ate dinner at TGIF.	(c) She was happy to see him. ➡ Was she happy to see him? Yes, she was. / No, she wasn't. (d) Why were you alone last night? I was alone because my parents went to the hospital.

Practice 1) Complete the sentences by filling in the blanks with the given words.

1. Last Saturday, I ________________ my bedroom. My sister did. (not, paint)

2. __________ Mary and Tom __________ physics before? (study)

3. Computers ________________ much more a few years ago! (cost)

4. Where ____________ you yesterday when I called you? (be)

5. When we ____________________ here, there wasn't a swimming pool. (live)

B. Present Perfect Tense

(a) She left Seoul.	Past tense
(b) She has left Seoul.	Present perfect tense

Sentence (a) simply tells what happened in the past (i.e., leaving Seoul). However, sentence (b) describes a past event (i.e., leaving Seoul) that has an impact on the present time (➡ She left Seoul, so she is not here now). When you explain something that happened in the past but has a connection to the present, you use have + pp form, which is called Present Perfect Tense.

(c) Song-ho lived in Busan for five years.	Past tense
(d) Song-ho has lived in Busan for five years.	Present perfect tense

Sentence (c) simply states a fact that Song-ho lived in Busan for five years in the past and he does **not** live here any longer. Sentence (d), however, indicates that Song-ho began to live in Busan 5 years ago and still lives there in the present and maybe in the future.

Grammar Tips!

과거에 일어난 일이 현재까지 영향을 미칠 때 영어에서는 현재완료 (have +pp) 시제를 사용한다. 현재완료시제는 한국어에는 없기 때문에 일반적으로 현재완료시제는 한국어로 과거시제처럼 번역이 된다. (A) I went to Jeju Island. (난 제주도에 갔었다.) 와 (B) I have been to Jeju Island. (난 제주도에 갔었다.) 하지만 두 문장의 의미는 차이가 있다. (A)는 '제주도에 갔었다' 라는 과거 경험 자체에 대한 기술이지만, (B)의 경우 '과거에 제주도에 간 것이 현재에 경험으로 남아있다' 라는 의미를 내포함으로 과거의 경험이 현재에까지 영향을 미치는 있는 것을 볼 수 있다. 영어권에서는 현재 완료 시제를 많이 사용하므로 의미를 잘 파악하여 적절한 상황에서 잘 사용하도록!

1. When to use present perfect tense

Sentence with Present Perfect Tense	Explanation
I have been to England before.	It describes an indefinite (=specific time is not given) event in the past (going to England) as an experience related to the present.
She has studied English for five years.	It describes an action (studying English) that began 5 years ago and it still continues.
They have just arrived at the airport.	It describes an event (arriving at the airport) that began in the past and completes very close to the present.
He has tried the medication three times.	It describes an action (trying the medication) that began in the past and is repeated from past till now.

Practice 2) Translate the following sentences into English.

1. 나는 10년 동안 영어를 공부했다.

2. Jane은 세살 때부터 Michigan 에서 살았다.

3. 나는 친구와 함께 서울 대공원에 가본 적이 있다. (Seoul Grand Park)

4. 그녀가 가장 좋아했던 수학선생님은 이제 떠나고 안 계시다.

2. How to make affirmative statements using present perfect tense

S + have/has + pp (past participle: regular verbs -d/ed)	S + have/has + pp (past participle: irregular verbs)
(a) I have watched the film several times. (b) He has cooked for the woman for five years.	(c) Mary has just come to his house. (d) They have gone to the new place. (e) I have been to the old castle.

3. How to make negative statements using present perfect tense

S + have/has + not + pp	S + have/has + not + been (be verb)
(a) I have watched the film several times. ➡ I have not watched the film several times. (b) She has not come to the party yet.	(c) I have been to the old castle. ➡ I have not been to the old castle. (d) He has not been very successful in his business.

4. How to make questions using present perfect tense

Have/Has + S+ pp?	Have/Has + S + been?
(a) Have you seen the cute girl living next door? Yes, I have. / No, I haven't (seen the cute girl living next door.). (b) Has he achieved his goals yet? Yes, he has. / No, he hasn't (achieved his goals).	(c) Have you ever been to France? Yes, I have. / No, I haven't (been to France). (d) Has Mr. Black been faithful to his boss? Yes, he has. / No, he hasn't (been faithful to his boss).

Practice 3) Complete the following sentences with proper words and expressions.

1. A: Have you ever been to the U.S.?
   B: No, ________________________________.

2. A: How long ________________________________?
   B: They have stayed here for five days.

3. I met him ten years ago and we became friends then. We are still good friends, so we ____________________ for ten years.

4. I met Susan three weeks ago, but ______________ her since then.

5. Useful time expressions in present perfect tense

for	Duration of time	I have lived in this house for 20 years.
since	Beginning point in the past	I have known him since I was nine years old. I have played the piano since I was young.
already, yet	At some time before now	I have already finished. A: Have you arrived yet? B: No, I have not arrived yet.
ever, never, before	At any time before now	A: Has he ever been to Korea? B: No, he has not ever been to Korea. (=No, he has never been to Korea.) I have tried the machine before. They have never studied hard.
recently, just	An unspecified, short time ago	The boss has just arrived. The market has recently closed.
once, many times	The number of times	She has taught the class several times.

Grammar Tips!

영어에서 yet, ever는 긍정문에 쓰이지 않고 부정문이나 의문문에서만 사용된다. 따라서 I have eaten yet. (X) 혹은 I have ever traveled. (X) 는 틀린 문장이다. Recently 와 just의 경우 구어체 영어 (informal English) 에서는 과거 시제와도 같이 사용한다. 예를 보면

Formal	Informal
I have just completed the project.	I just finished the project.
Mary has recently earned her degree.	Mary recently got her degree.

Practice 4) Correct or Incorrect?

Read the following sentences. If the sentence is correct, circle C. If it is not correct, circle IC. If you circle IC, correct the mistake.

1. She has not eaten ice cream for five years. (C IC)

☞ Correction:

2. I have been to France in 2004. (C IC)

☞ Correction:

3. Until the 1960s, Korea has received aid from other countries. (C IC)

☞ Correction:

4. Mary has never been to Disneyland although she lived in Los Angeles.

(C IC)

☞ Correction:

5. Dragons have fascinated us for many centuries. (C IC)

☞ Correction:

6. I lived with Komodo people while I have been there. (C IC)

☞ Correction:

Grammar Tips!

위에서 소개했던 대로 현재 완료 시제에 자주 쓰이는 시간 표현이 있는가 하면 (already, just, ever, since, for), 현재완료 시제와 함께 쓸 수 없는 표현들이 있다. 예를 들어 I have watched the movie two days ago. (X) 라고 쓰면 틀린 표현이 되는데 이것은 'two days ago' 가 분명한 과거의 시간을 나타내기 때문이다. 이와 같이 현재 완료형은 과거의 어느 특정한 때를 나타내는 시간 표현과 함께 쓸 수 없다. (three weeks ago, yesterday, last week, in 2005)

Unit in a Nutshell

- In describing something that happened in the past, use simple past tense.
- To make a past form of a regular verb, add –(e)d to the verb (cook ➡ cooked). With an irregular verb, memorize the past form of the verb (go ➡ went, take ➡ took).
- In describing something that happened in the past but has a connection to the present, use present perfect tense.
- With specific time adverbs in the past, don't use present perfect tense (yesterday, last week, in 2005).

Practice 5) Translate the sentences (English–Korean/Korean–English).

1. I've just spoken to Peter. I phoned him five minutes ago.

2. Mr. Lee는 회의 때 늦는 법이 없는데 오늘은 15분 지각 했다.

3. She's always been a vegetarian. She hasn't ever eaten meat since she saw a shocking scene at the butcher shop on the corner.

4. 김 교수님의 수업을 듣고 나서부터 난 철학에 관심이 생겼다.

Writing in Action

Task 1.

Complete the following story by filling in each blank with a proper form of the word.

My Special Weekend

My hometown, Hadong, is not a big city, nor a famous tourist place. Nevertheless, this is a very special place to me because there are many people I love and great memories I ____________(cherish) since my childhood.

I ____________(go) to Hadong last weekend. The city ____________(change) a lot since I ____________(leave) the town after high school. Small playgrounds and rice paddies ____________ (turn) into high rise buildings and nicely paved roads now. As soon as I ____________ (arrive), I ____________ (visit) my grandmother's house. She ____________ (age) a bit. She looks as young and beautiful as she used to be. After having lunch with her, I ____________ (call) my old friends to hang out. We ____________ (be) friends for more than 15 years now. Yang-su is, among them, my best friend. We ________ (be) in the same class in high school for two years. When we were preparing for the college entrance exam, we ____________ (promise) each other to go to the same university. He

____________ (want) to study physics, and I liked history. We applied for the same school, but he ______________ (make) it. Later, however, he changed his mind and decided to go to school near my hometown instead of coming to Seoul. He is majoring in law instead of physics. He wants to be a lawyer and so _________________ (prepare) for the bar exam for two years. We talked a lot about our campus life, new friends, and our goals. Although I ______________ (feel) very sad to say good bye to my friends, I ______ (be) very happy to see them again and know that I have wonderful friends with whom I can share my life for a long time.

Task 2.

Becoming a storyteller: writing an autobiography

Think for a moment and write about your life as a story. In your writing, try to use two verb tenses (simple past and present prefect) to express what you did and how you have lived. Describe major events of your life and explain how such experiences have influenced you in the present time.

To generate ideas for the writing, first ask yourself the following questions.

(1) What is some background information about yourself?

(2) What were some important events in your life?
What happened?
Who was involved in the event?
What have you learned from this experience?

(3) How have these events/experiences influenced you?

(Draw or insert a picture to highlight your story)

Unit 2 Answer Key

Test yourself! (p. 23)

(1) A: Who did you go there with?

B: I went there with my friend Jeff.

(2) A: Did she like moving to the new school?

B: No, she didn't.

(3) John's mother believed that John went to hospital after school. However, it was not true. John did not go to hospital after school.

(4) They carry a lot of boxes every day, but they did not carry boxes yesterday due to heavy rain.

(5) A: Did he go to the party or to the library last night?

B: Well, he went to the library. He had to study for the final exam.

Practice 1 (p. 25)

1. Last Saturday, I didn't paint my bedroom. My sister did.
2. Did Mary and Tom study physics before?
3. Computers cost much more a few years ago!
4. Where were you yesterday when I called you?
5. When we lived here, there wasn't a swimming pool.

Practice 2 (p. 28)

1. I have studied English for 10 years.
2. Jane has lived in Michigan since she was three.
3. I have been to Seoul Grand Park with friends.
4. Her favorite math teacher has gone/left.

Practice 3 (p. 29)

1. A: Have you ever been to the U.S.?

   B: No, I haven't (ever been to the U.S.) / No, I have never been to the U.S.
2. A: How long have they stayed here?

   B: They have stayed here for five days.
3. I met him ten years ago and we became friends then. We are still good friends, so we have been friends for ten years.
4. I met Susan three weeks ago but haven't seen her since then.

Practice 4 (p. 31)

1. C
2. IC : have been → went
3. IC : has received → received
4. C
5. C
6. IC : have been → was

Practice 5 (p. 32)

1. 나 지금 피터랑 막 통화했어. 내가 5분전에 전화했거든.

2. Mr. Lee has never been late for meetings, but he was 15 minutes late today.

3. 그녀는 늘 채식주의자였어. 구석진 길에 있던 정육점에서 끔직한 광경을 본 이후로는 고기를 전혀 먹지 않지.

4. I have become interested in philosophy since I took Professor Kim's class.

Task 1 (p. 33)

My Special Weekend

My hometown, Hadong, is not a big city, nor famous tourist place. Nevertheless, this is a very special place to me because there are many people I love and great memories I **have cherished** since my childhood.

I **went** to Hadong last weekend. The city **has changed** a lot since I **left** the town after high school. Small playgrounds and rice paddies **have turned** into high rise buildings and nicely paved roads now. As soon as I **arrived**, I **visited** my grandmother's house. She **hasn't aged** a bit. She looks as young and beautiful as she used to be. After having lunch with her, I **called** my old friends to hang out. We **have been** friends for more than 15 years now. Yang-su is, among them, my best friend. We **were** in the same class in high school for two years. When we were preparing for the college entrance exam, we **promised** to each other to go to the same university. He **wanted** to study physics, and I liked history. We applied for the same school, but he **did not make** it. Later, however, he changed his mind and decided to go to school near my hometown instead of coming to Seoul. He is majoring in law instead of physics. He wants to be a lawyer and so **has prepared** for the bar exam for two years. We talked a lot about our campus life, new friends, and our goals. Although I **felt** very sad to say good bye to my friends, I **was** very happy to see them again and know that I have wonderful friends with whom I can share my life for a long time.

Unit 3 Articles

Test yourself!

Unscramble the given words in a correct order.

(1) ____

(a, your, friend, is, Kim, vegetarian) (Question)

(2) ____

(you, did, like, food, the, at, party, yesterday, the) (Question)

(3) ____________________ ____________________

(whale, is, a, not, a, fish) (is, a, it, mammal)

(4) ____

(dollars, the, trip, almost, cost, a, hundred)

(5) ____

(good, had, old, the, man, and, woman, life, a)

Grammar Tips!

영어는 한국어와 달리 명사를 사용할 때는 항상 관사를 염두에 두어야 한다. 즉, 문장에서 사용되는 명사가 1) 셀 수 있는 명사인지, 셀 수 없는 명사인지, 2) 단수인지 복수인지(복수 명사인 경우 -(s)를 붙여 복수형을 만들거나 불규칙 명사형을 기억하고 있어야 한다), 3) 일반적인 이야기를 하는지, 특정한 것에 관한 이야기를 하는 지에 따라 부정관사 a/an, 정관사 the, 또는 관사를 사용하지 않기도 한다.

A. Indefinite Articles

(a) Use *a* with singular nouns.

a week	a book	a person	a house
a tables (x)	a parents (x)	a children (x)	a sports (x)

(b) Use *a* with count(able) nouns.

a box	a job	a holiday	a teacher
a work (x)	a traffic (x)	a water (x)	a furniture (x)

As you see in the examples of (a) and (b), indefinite articles a/an are related to singular, count(able) nouns.

(c) Use *an* with words that begin with vowel sound : */a, e, i, o, u./*

an elephant	an apple	an idiot	an opinion	an umbrella
an cat (x)	an test (x)	an beach (x)		

(d) Use *an* in front of the words that begin with *h* if the *h* is silent.

an hour	an hono(u)r	an honest man
a hospital	a hope	

(e) Use *a* in front of the words that begin with *eu* or *u* if the first sound is pronounced */ju:/*.

a university	a European company
a ugly face (x)	an universe (x)

The examples of (c), (d), and (e) show when to use the unmarked indefinite article 'an'. You can use 'an' with the following nouns pronounced with vowel sounds (a, e, i, o, u). In the case of 'silent h' like the examples of (d), you should use 'an.' Also, in the case of words beginning with the letter 'u' and they are pronounced */ju:/*, you can not use the indefinite article 'an'.

(f) Use *a/an* when you are talking about a person or thing for the first time.
There is a man at the door.
I need to buy a new T-shirt.

(g) Use *a/an* to talk about jobs.
My father is an engineer now, but he was a soldier before.
I worked as a secretary last summer. This year I want to be a shop assistant.

You use indefinite articles 'a' or 'an' when you talk about a person or a thing for the first time as in (f) and when you talk about jobs as in (g).

(h) Use *a/an* instead of one with some numbers.

a hundred dollars	half a kilo	a million people
an hour	a thousand times	a liter of water

(i) Use *a/an* to replace 'per.'
How often do you go to the cinema? About once a month.
How much are these potatoes? $2.50 a kilo.
Heidi works eight hours a day, six days a week.

The indefinite article 'a' is used as 'one' (하나, 한 개) in numbers as in (h) or 'per' (~당, ~마다) as in (i).

Grammar Tips!

영어에서는 식사 이름 (breakfast, lunch, and dinner) 앞에는 관사를 쓰지 않는다. What did you have for dinner? (저녁 식사로 무엇을 먹었습니까?) 또는 What time is breakfast? (아침 식사는 몇 시입니까?)의 예문처럼 관사 'a/an' 또는 'the'를 쓰지 않는다. 하지만 형용사를 써서 수식하는 경우는 부정관사 'a/an'이 함께 쓰인다. 예를 들면 I had a delicious lunch.처럼 delicious라는 형용사를 쓸 경우는 부정관사 'a'를 써야 한다.

Practice 1) Complete the sentences with the proper article if necessary.

1. They are reading ________ story about ________ man and ________ young girl.

2. A: What's that?
   B: It's ________ hamster.

3. Do you have ________ orange pen?

4. I'm looking for ________ supermarket.

5. A: What do you do?
   B: I'm ________ university student.

6. He was ________ socialist, not ________ communist.

7. She said that she was living in ________ old apartment in the center of Chicago.

B. Definite Article

(a) Use *the* with a singular noun when the person you are speaking to knows which person or thing you are talking about:
I left the keys on the kitchen table.
The president is coming next month.
Who is the man next to Mary?
I had a book and a magazine with me. I read the book first.
She bought a new shirt and a tie for her husband. The tie was very expensive.

(b) Use *the* with a plural noun when the person you are speaking to knows which group of people or things you are talking about:
Where are the children?
He bought two shirts. The shirts were quite cheap.
Have you washed the cups and saucers?

You use the definite article 'the' with a singular noun and also a plural noun when the person you are speaking to knows which person or group of people or thing(s) you are talking about.

(c) Use *the* when you are talking about a system or service.
I spoke to her on the phone yesterday.
I heard it on the radio.
Can you turn off the television (=the television set), please?
cf. I watch television a lot.

You can use 'the' when you are talking about a system or service. However, when you say 'I watch TV a lot,' it means you watch a lot of TV programs. It does not mean the television set, so you do not need the article 'the'.

(d) Use *the* with a singular noun when you want to make a general statement about something.
The tiger is a very dangerous animal.
My favorite flower is the tulip.

You do not use 'the' when you use a plural noun to make a general statement, or when you make a general statement about an uncountable noun.
Gold is a metal. (O) / The gold is a metal. (x)
Apples are my favorite fruit. (O) / The apples are my favorite fruit. (x)

Grammar Tips!

일반적인 사실을 얘기할 경우에는 다음과 같이 관사를 사용할 수 있다.

1) *A tiger* is a dangerous animal.

2) *Tigers* are dangerous animals.

3) *The tiger* is a dangerous animal.

4) *The tigers* are dangerous animals.*

1)-3)번 문장들은 호랑이에 대한 일반적인 이야기를 할 때 쓰고, 4)번 문장은 특정한 호랑이를 지칭할 때 쓰인다.

(e) I go to school every day (to study).
(f) I went to the school (to meet my friends) last Sunday.

When some words of place are used as their purpose, you do not use 'the' with the nouns. For example, think about schools and hospitals. People go to school to learn or study. Likewise, people go to hospitals to get a treatment. So if you say 'I go to school every day,' as in (e), it means you go to school to study. On the other hand, if you say "I went to **the** school (to meet my friends) last Sunday,' as in (f), it means you went to **the** school with a purpose other than studying because schools don't usually have classes open on Sundays.

(g) Use ***the*** with the names of only a few countries, with the names of rivers, oceans, and seas, and with the names of mountian ranges, but **not mountains!**

the Czech Republic the United Arab Emirates
the Dominican Republic the Philippines the Netherlands
the Nile the Pacific Ocean the Alps the Andes
the Mount Seorak (x)

Grammar Tips!

국가명, 산맥, 강 등의 고유명사에 정관사 the를 사용하는 경우가 있으므로 기억해야 한다.

(h) Do ***not*** use ***the*** with titled names, the names of cities, the names of continents, and the names of most countries.

We met the Mr. Chang. (X) She lives in the Paris. (X)
We went on a trip to the Europe. (X) He lives in the China. (X)

Practice 2) Complete the sentences with the proper article if necessary.

1. This morning I bought ______ newspaper and ________ magazine. ______ newspaper is in my bag, but I can't remember where I put ______ magazine.

2. I saw ______ accident this morning. ______ car crashed into ______ tree. ______ driver of ______ car wasn't hurt, but ______ car was badly damaged.

3. A: Where did you have _____ lunch?
   B: We went to ______ Italian restaurant.

4. There are two cars parked outside: ______ white one and ______ black one. ______ white one belongs to my neighbor; I don't know who ______ owner of ______ black one is.

5. A: Did you have ______ nice holiday?
   B: Yes, it was ______ best holiday I've ever had.

6. A: Would you like ______ piece of ______ cake I made yesterday?
   B: Yes, that'd be nice. But just ______ small piece.

7. A: What time are you going to ______ match tomorrow?
   B: I've told you ______ hundred times, at two o'clock.

8. ______ B(b)eef is a kind of ______ meat.

Practice 3) Correct the errors in each sentence.

1. The earthquakes are rare in central Africa.

☞ Correction:

2. Last week I read book about the life of Gandhi.

☞ Correction:

3. I like listening to the music when I come home.

☞ Correction:

4. Lake is a body of water which is smaller than a sea but larger than a pond.

☞ Correction:

5. During our vacation in Miami, we walked along beach in front of our hotel and looked at an ocean.

☞ Correction:

6. Well, I drive to my office in a city center five days the week, but I don't use my car much on weekends.

☞ Correction:

Practice 4) Translate the Korean sentences into English using proper articles.

1. 나는 이번 학기에 역사 과목을 수강하고 있다. (take, history, semester)

2. 록키 산맥은 캐나다와 미국에 위치하고 있다. (Rocky Mountains, locate)

3. 좋은 책은 인생의 친구이다. (good, book, friend, life)

4. A: 커피가 어디 있지? (where, coffee)

   B: 싱크대 옆에 찬장에 있어. (in, cupboard, next to, sink)

Unit in a Nutshell

- The indefinite article 'a/an' is used to introduce a thing for the first time.
- The definite article 'the' is used to indicate something that has been already mentioned or introduced or something that both parties already know.
- Some usages of articles are conventional (i.e. not following a specific rule); therefore, the best way to learn how to use articles is through exposure to many types of English texts.

Practice 5) Correct or Incorrect?

Read the following sentences. If it is correct, circle C. If it is not correct, circle IC. If you circle IC, correct the mistake.

1. She read the letters that had arrived that morning. (C IC)

   ☞ Correction:

2. I want to put some money into my bank account, so I'm going to bank this afternoon. (C IC)

   ☞ Correction:

3. I'm trying to learn Japanese. I have lesson tomorrow. (C IC)

   ☞ Correction:

4. They made a angry speech against government. (C IC)

   ☞ Correction:

5. Doctors say that exercise is good for everybody. (C IC)

   ☞ Correction:

6. Yesterday, I was sitting on a 6 o'clock train when I saw strange man walking along the platform. (C IC)

   ☞ Correction:

Writing in Action

Task 1.

Complete the following story by filling in the blanks with proper articles.

A Picture of a Family

There are four adults and three children in this family. ______ children are Dae-han, sixteen years old, Min-kuk, ten years old, and Man-se, who is seven years old. Their parents are Dae-gil and Young-sim. ______ other adults are Yoo-jung and Soon-ja, who are Dae-gil's parents. They live near Ulsan, a large city in ______ south-east of Korea.

On ______ weekday mornings, everyone gets up early. Dae-gil works for a company which makes ______ cars. He leaves at seven o'clock. He likes to avoid ______ rush hour, he says. Young-sim suspects that he likes to avoid having breakfast with ______ children, who are very noisy.

Min-Kuk and Man-se catch ______ school bus at eight-fifteen. Dae-han is at ______ art high school, studying fine art. He lives away from ______ home during the semester, so he avoids ______ noise, too.

Their grandparents work as ______ volunteers at ______ community center near their house. They leave home at 10. When they leave, Young-sim, who is ______ housewife, starts cleaning the house and doing the laundry. After that, she has some time to enjoy ______ cup of coffee before ______ lunch.

Task 2.

Write one or two paragraphs to describe your room. Make sure that you use articles correctly in your writing.

My Room

Unit 3 Answer Key

Test yourself! (p. 39)

(1) Is your friend Kim a vegetarian?

(2) Did you like the food at the party yesterday?

(3) A whale is not a fish. It is a mammal.

(4) The trip cost almost a hundred dollars.

(5) The old man and woman had a good life.

Practice 1) (p. 42)

1. They are reading a story about a man and a young girl.
2. A: What's that?
   B: It's a hamster.
3. Do you have an orange pen?
4. I'm looking for a supermarket.
5. A: What do you do?
   B: I'm a university student.
6. He was a socialist, not a communist.
7. She said that she was living in an old apartment in the center of Chicago.

Practice 2) (p. 46)

1. This morning I bought a newspaper and a magazine. The newspaper is in my bag, but I can't remember where I put the magazine.
2. I saw an accident this morning. A car crashed into a tree. The driver

of the car wasn't hurt, but the car was badly damaged.

3. A: Where did you have lunch? (No article)

   B: We went to an Italian restaurant.

4. There are two cars parked outside: a white one and a black one. The white one belongs to my neighbor; I don't know who the owner of the black one is.

5. A: Did you have a nice holiday?

   B: Yes, it was the best holiday I've ever had.

6. A: Would you like a piece of the cake I made yesterday?

   B: Yes, that'd be nice. But just a small piece.

7. A: What time are you going to the match tomorrow?

   B: I've told you a hundred times, at two o' clock.

8. Beef is a kind of meat. (No article)

Practice 3) (p. 47)

1. Earthquakes are rare in central Africa.
2. Last week I read a book about the life of Gandhi.
3. I like listening to music when I come home.
4. A lake is a body of water which is smaller than a sea but larger than a pond.
5. During our vacation in Miami, we walked along the beach in front of our hotel and looked at the ocean.
6. Well, I drive to my office in the city center five days a week, but I don' t use my car much on weekends.

Practice 4) (p. 48)

1. I'm taking a history course this semester.
2. The Rocky Mountains are located in Canada and the United States.
3. A good book is a friend for life.
4. A: Where is the coffee?

   B: It's in the cupboard next to the sink.

Practice 5) (p. 49)

1. C
2. IC : to bank → to the bank
3. IC : have lesson → have a lesson
4. IC : a angry → an angry, government → the government
5. C
6. IC : on a 6 o'clock → on the 6 o'clock, strange man → a strange man

Task 1. (p. 50)

A Picture of a Family

There are four adults and three children in this family. The children are Dae-han, sixteen years old, Min-kuk, ten years old, and Man-se, who is seven years old. Their parents are Dae-gil and Young-sim. The other adults are Yoo-jung and Soon-ja, who are Dae-gil's parents. They live near Ulsan, a large city in the south-east of Korea.

On – weekday mornings, everyone gets up early. Dae-gil works for a company which makes – cars. He leaves at seven o'clock. He likes to avoid – rush hour, he says. Young-sim suspects that he likes to avoid having breakfast with the children, who are very noisy.

Min-Kuk and Man-se catch the school bus at eight-fifteen. Dae-han is at an art high school, studying fine art. He lives away from – home during the semester, so he avoids the noise, too.

Their grandparents work as – volunteers at the/a community center near their house. They leave home at 10. When they leave, Young-sim, who is a housewife, starts cleaning the house and doing the laundry. After that, she has some time to enjoy a cup of coffee before – lunch.

Unit 4 Sentence Patterns: Simple Sentences and Compound Sentences

Test yourself!

Combine the two sentences into one sentence.

(1) Mangoes have pits. Peaches and plums have pits.

____

(2) Inflammation may cause some discomfort. Itching may cause some discomfort.

____

(3) The dog chased the car down the alley. The policeman chased the car down the alley.

____

(4) We arrived on campus Sunday. We located our dorm room. We unloaded our car and started to settle in.

____

Grammar Tips!

'He is a student.' 와 같이 주어와 동사가 1개씩 포함되어 있는 기본적인 영어문장을 단문(simple sentences)이라고 하고, I want to go to the party, but my friend wants to stay at home.' 와 같이 단문 2개가 등위접속사로 연결되어 있는 문장은 중문(compound sentences)라고 한다.

A. Simple Sentences

(a) Jane is a great dancer. (S+V)
(b) Minhee and Jake met each other in New York. (SS+V)
(c) He went out and closed the door. (S+VV)
(d) Sean and his friends played games and drank coffee. (SS+VV)

A simple sentence is a sentence with one clause (subject + verb) that expresses a complete idea. A subject describes the agent (who or what) of the sentence, and a verb explains the action or condition of the sentence. A sentence may have a complement (보어) or object (목적어) depending on the verb in the sentence. In addition, a simple sentence can have either compound subject (SS) or compound verb (VV) as you can see in sentences (b) to (d).

1. Sentence types

There are five different types of simple sentences, and each type is decided by whether the verb requires a complement or object.

Type (1): Subject + Verb			
	Subject	Verb	
(a)	John	swam	in the pond yesterday.
(b)	Sarah	came	to the party after work.
(c)	I	came	home right after school.

This is the simplest type of a sentence. It consists of a subject and verb, and time or place expressions can be added. In type (1) sentences, you use an intransitive verb (자동사), which does not take an object. As you see in (a) to (c), the underlined parts are expressions of time or place. These expressions are often made up of prepositional phrases (전치사구) or adverbs.

Type (2): Subject + Verb + Complement

	Subject	Verb	Complement
(a)	My younger brother	is	smart. (adjective)
(b)	My father	is	a system engineer. (noun phrase)

The second sentence type is composed of S + V + C. A complement is a word or group of words that describe or rename the subject. Complements follow a linking verb. A linking verb is a verb that does not express action, but simply links the subject to the complement. Complements are often adjectives (e.g. smart) or nouns (e.g. a system engineer).

Type (3): Subject + Verb + Object

	Subject	Verb	Object
(a)	I	ate	a huge helping of turkey on Thanksgiving.
(b)	She	lost	the addresses of old friends.

Some verbs require an object to complete the idea in the sentence. These verbs are called transitive verbs (타동사). The object answers 'what' of the verb. For example, I ate 'what'? I ate 'a huge helping of turkey' as in (a).

Type (4): Subject + Verb + Indirect Object (IO) + Direct Object (DO)

	Subject	Verb	IO	DO
(a)	Mary	gave	John	a letter.
	(= Mary gave a letter to John.)			
(b)	Mama	knits	everyone	a new sweater on Christmas.
	(= Mama knits a new sweater for everyone on Christmas.)			
(c)	The elders	tell	the children	stories of the tribe.

There are verbs that take two objects: 1) one is an indirect object (IO) that usually describes the person who receives the action; 2) the other is direct object (DO). If you change the order of IO and DO, you need to add a preposition 'to' or 'for' according to the verb in the sentence.

Type (5): Subject + Verb + Object + Object Complement

	Subject	Verb	O	OC
(a)	We	elected	Clinton	president in the last presidential election.
(b)	He	named	the dog	Happy.

This sentence type requires an object and object complement. An object complement describes more information about the object, not the subject, in a sentence.

Grammar Tips!

영어의 타동사는 전치사 없이 바로 목적어를 취한다 (3, 4, 5형식동사). 예를 들어, discuss, resemble, marry 등이다. 이러한 타동사들은 '~에게, ~을, ~에 대하여, ~와' 등으로 해석되며, 전치사가 필요없다.

예 1) to discuss the plan (O), to discuss about the plan (x)
예 2) to answer the question (O), to answer to the question (x)
예 3) to regret the error (O), to regret for the error (x)
예 4) to resemble her father (O), to resemble like her father (x)

2. Subject-Verb agreement

(1) When you write a sentence, there is a basic but very important rule. That is, the subject and verb must agree in number. Look at the following

examples.

(a) My sister is very intelligent. (singular–단수)
(b) My sisters are very intelligent. (plural–복수)

(2) Some words (each, every, one of) always take singular verbs.

(a) Each book is a different color.
(b) Every apartment has a balcony.
(c) One of the pupils is missing.

(3) In the case of quantity expressions (all of, a lot of, some of, most of, none of), you use a singular verb when an uncountable noun comes after a quantifier. When a countable noun comes after the quantifier, you need to use plural verbs.

(a) All of my time is spent in the library. (singular)
All of the flowers in this garden are beautiful. (plural)

(b) A lot of the work was too easy. (singular)
A lot of people were angry. (plural)

(c) Some of the money was missing. (singular)
Some of the students were missing. (plural)

(d) Most of the ice was melted. (singular)
Most of the students in my English class ask questions. (plural)

(e) None of the fruit is fresh. (singular)
None of the apples are fresh. (plural)

(4) When you use the expressions 'most of', 'some of', or 'all of', be careful to add the article 'the' before the noun. If not, you can use these words without 'of'. Look at the following examples.

(a) Most of students have fun on Saturday nights. (X)
Most students have fun on Saturday nights. (O)
Most of the students in my college have fun on Saturday nights. (O)

(b) Some of people don't care what they do in public. (X)
Some people don't care what they do in public. (O)
Some of the people I know don't care what they do in public. (O)

(c) All of girls want to meet Tom Cruise. (X)
All girls want to meet Tom Cruise. (O)
All (of) the girls want to meet Tom Cruise. (O)

Grammar Tips!

'~of the'가 없는 경우에는 일반적인 모든 사람을 뜻하고, '~of the'가 있는 경우에는 특정그룹의 사람들을 뜻한다. 예를 들어 (b)의 'most students'는 대부분의 일반적인 학생들을 뜻하고, (c)의 'most of the students in my college'는 우리 대학에 다니는 대부분의 학생들을 뜻한다.

(5) 'A number of' vs. 'the number of'

(a) A number of students <u>are</u> interested in English writing. (plural)
(b) The number of students <u>is</u> forty. (singular)

'A number of' (많은) means 'many' and a plural verb follows as in (a). 'The number of (~의 수)+ plural N' is followed by a singular verb as you see in (b).

Practice 1) Complete the sentences with 'be verb'.

1. Most of the children in this school _____ under 12 years old.

2. Some of this money _____ yours.

3. None of my friends _____ interested in painting.

4. We can't find any place for the study group. All of the classrooms _____ full.

5. Not all my cousins _____ at the wedding last week.

3. Paired connectors

In English, you can connect two words using more than one connecting word. This is called 'paired connectors' (상관접속사). Look at the examples in the following.

(a) Both my mother and my sister are here.
→ Both A and B + V (plural)

(b) Not only my mother but also my sister is here.
Not only my sister but also my parents are here.
→ not only A ~ but also B + V (agree with B)

(c) Either my mother or my sisters love to cook.
Either my sisters or my mother loves to cook.
→ either A ~ or B + V (agree with B)

(d) Neither my mother nor my sister is here.
Neither my sister nor my parents are here.
→ neither A ~ nor B + V (agree with B)

(e) I as well as she am interested in music.
→ A as well as B + V (agree with A)

When you use a paired connector, you need to be careful with S-V agreement. For example, when you use both A and B, you need a plural verb. When using not only A but also B, either A or B, or neither A nor B, you use a verb in agreement with the noun B as you see in (b) to (d). However, with A as well as B, you need to use a verb that agrees with A as you see in (e).

Practice 2) Fill in each blank using a proper form of 'be' verb.

1. Both the teacher and the student ________ here.

2. Neither the teacher nor the student ________ here.

3. Not only the teacher but also the students _______ here.

4. Either the teacher or the students ________ planning to come.

5. She as well as I _____ not afraid of making mistakes.

B. Compound Sentences

A compound sentence is a sentence that has two independent clauses joined by a comma and a coordinating conjunction. (등위접속사)

(a) Japan imports oil, and Saudi Arabia imports vegetables.
(b) Sue watched TV, but Ben studied English.
(c) Jane does not love Jack, so she will not marry him.

1. Seven coordinating conjunctions

In English, there are only seven coordinating conjunctions: for, and, nor, but, or, yet, so (FANBOYS). When you connect two independent clauses with a coordinating connector, use a comma before the connector.

Conjunction	Function	Example
for	expressing reason	I am a little hungry, for I didn't have breakfast this morning.
and	adding similar ideas	John likes to fish, and Jane loves to eat fish.
nor	connecting two negative clauses	She does not eat meat, nor does she drink milk.(V + S 어순 도치에 주의!)
but	showing contrast	I like to eat fish, but I don't know how to catch them.
or	expressing choice	Do you prefer to have lunch, or do you want to drink coffee first?
yet	showing partial contrast (unexpected)	It was cold, yet the children went out to play.
so	showing a result	I did not eat breakfast this morning, so I am a little hungry.

Grammar Tips!

등위접속사는 단어와 단어, 구와 구, 절과 절을 대등하게 이어주는 역할을 한다. 단, 접속사 so와 for는 절과 절만을 연결하는 기능이 있다.

예 1) He prepared eggs and bacon for breakfast. (단어와 단어를 연결)

예 2) They enjoy playing the piano and climbing mountains. (구와 구를 연결)

예 3) Wendy cut her finger, so she went to a doctor. (절과 절만 연결 가능)

Practice 3) Complete the sentences using a proper coordinating connector and punctuation.

1. John is watching a movie __________ Ann is eating popcorn.

2. I bought a newspaper ________ I didn't read it.

3. Do you want me to come with you _________ should I wait here?

4. It is morning ____________ it is still dark.

5. Mary needed to buy a gift _________ it was her mother's birthday.

Practice 4) Read the two sentences. Write C for a cause and R for a result on the line next to the sentence. Then combine them into a compound sentence without changing the order of two sentences. Use a proper connector.

1. a. _______ I was thirsty.
   b. _______ I drank three glasses of water.
   → ____

2. a. _______ We took the cat to the vet.
   b. _______ The cat was very sick.
   → ____

3. a. ________ The plane did not leave on time.

b. ________ We arrived at our destination late.

→ ____

2. Compound sentences with a semicolon (;)

Another way to make a compound sentence is to join the two clauses with a semicolon. First, look at the examples that use a semicolon to connect the two parts. A semicolon can alone connect two clauses when the relationship between the two parts is so clear that you do not need a connector.

(a) Tom loves Erica; she loves him, too.
(b) Jack loves Jane; she loves Ronald.
(c) Jane does not love Jack; she will not marry him.

Notice that the first word after the semicolon is not capitalized because this is NOT the beginning of a sentence.

3. Compound sentences with a conjunctive adverb

(a) Jack didn't study; therefore, he failed the test.
(b) Sue wanted to meet him; however, she could not find where he was.
(c) Michelle loves to cook; similarly, her sister likes to cook.

A third way to make a compound sentence is to join two clauses with a conjunctive adverb (접속부사). When you use a conjunctive adverb to combine two parts, add a semicolon + conjunctive adverb + comma between two clauses.

(a) Jack didn't study. Therefore, he failed the test.
(b) Jack didn't study. He, therefore, failed the test.
(c) Jack didn't study, and therefore, he failed the test.
(d) Jack didn't study, therefore he failed the test. (X)

In other cases, a conjunctive adverb can come at the beginning of a sentence or between a subject and a verb as you see in (a) and (b) above. Notice that a conjunctive adverb alone **cannot** connect two clauses as in (d).

Commonly used conjunctive adverbs

Conjunctive Adverb (접속부사)	Meaning
nevertheless, nonetheless	양보 (그럼에도 불구하고)
otherwise	조건, 가정 (그렇지 않으면)
on the other hand, by contrast, however, on the contrary	대조 (반대로)
moreover, also, besides, in addition, furthermore	첨가 (게다가, 또한)
therefore, thus, consequently, accordingly, hence, as a result	결과 (따라서, 그래서)
likewise, similarly	비교 (비슷하게, 마찬가지로)

Practice 5) Translate the sentences into English. Write a compound sentence using a conjunctive adverb in each sentence.

1. 그는 가난함에도 불구하고 무척 행복하다.

2. Jane은 수영 시합에서 최선을 다해서 결국 금메달을 땄다.

3. 오늘 밤에 출발하지 않으면 그 회의에 늦게 될 거야.

4. 그녀도 그녀의 어머니처럼 요리를 잘한다.

Unit in a Nutshell

- There are five types of simple sentences in English depending on the type of a main verb. (SV, SVC, SVO, SVIODO, SVOC)
- Subject-Verb agreement rule needs to be kept in any sentence.
- Compound sentences are made by using coordinating conjunctions: for, and, nor, but, or, yet, so.
- Conjunctive adverbs are also used to make a compound sentence. In this case, semi-colon (;) is used to connect two clauses.

Practice 6) Identify the following sentence. Write 'S' for simple sentence and 'C' for compound sentence. For a compound sentence, rewrite the sentence using a conjunctive adverb.

1. The Japanese flag is red and white, and the Canadian flag is also red and white.

____

2. Japan and Canada have the same two colors in their flags.

____

3. The weather is bad, so the plane cannot take off on time.

____

4. It is extremely hot in this room without an air conditioner.

____

Practice 7) Correct or Incorrect?

Read the following sentences. If it is correct, circle C. If it is not correct, circle IC. For IC, correct the mistake.

1. Most of my friends in our class are very nice. (C IC)

☞ Correction:

2. Some of questions on the exam were very easy. (C IC)

☞ Correction:

3. Either Marie or you are going to be transferred to the Washington branch. (C IC)

☞ Correction:

4. Clearly, not everybody in the manufacturing or routine service industries are promoted to the highest position of responsibility. (C IC)

☞ Correction:

5. The number of applicants with work experience is now 60 percent, up 10 percent from last year's survey. (C IC)

☞ Correction:

Writing in Action

Task 1.

Complete the following passage by choosing the correct verb or filling in the blanks with proper words.

Education: A Reflection of Society

In contrast, the Japanese value education highly. They place such importance on it that most of the students (complete/completes) not only primary school __________ high school. Public schools are all both free _______ egalitarian; __________, all students (is/are) considered equal, ______ they learn the same material. For social reasons, it's important for a student to receive a university degree and a degree from 'the right university', ________ all of the students (has/have) to go through 'examination hell.' There are difficult exams for entrance to all universities, to many of the better primary and secondary schools, and even to some kindergartens! A lot of Japanese students (need/needs) great discipline. Because of studying, a number of students (do/does) not have time for hobbies, ________ do they enjoy their social life. Results of these exams affect the entire family, _______ there is high status or social position for the whole family when the children have high test scores.

(from Baker, L. R. et al. 2003. Interactions 2: Integrated Skills. McGraw-Hill)

Task 2.

Write about the country to which you want to travel. Before writing the paragraph, think about the following questions. Use simple sentences and compound sentences with coordinating conjunctions or conjunctive adverbs in your writing.

To generate ideas for the writing, first ask yourself the following questions.

(1) Which country would you like to travel to?

(2) Why do you want to travel to that specific country?

(3) What do you want to do in that country?

Unit 4 Answer Key

Test yourself! (p. 57)

(1) Mangoes, peaches, and plums have pits.

(2) Inflammation and itching may cause some discomfort.

(3) The dog and the policeman chased the car down the alley.

(4) We arrived on campus Sunday, located our dorm room, unloaded our car, and started to settle in.

Practice 1) (p. 63)

1. Most of the children in this school are under 12 years old.
2. Some of this money is yours.
3. None of my friends are interested in paintings.
4. We can't find any place for study group. All of the classrooms are full.
5. Not all my cousins were at the wedding last week.

Practice 2) (p. 64)

1. Both the teacher and the student are here.
2. Neither the teacher nor the student is here.
3. Not only the teacher but also the students are here.
4. Either the teacher or the students are planning to come.
5. She as well as I is not afraid of making mistakes.

Practice 3) (p. 66)

1. John is watching a movie, and Ann is eating popcorn.
2. I bought a newspaper, but I didn't read it.
3. Do you want me to come with you, or should I wait here?
4. It is morning, yet it is still dark.
5. Mary needed to buy a gift, for it was her mother's birthday.

Practice 4) (p. 66)

1. a. C b. R

   → I was thirsty, so I drank three glasses of water.
2. a. R b. C

   → We took the cat to the vet, for the cat was very sick.
3. a. C b. R

   → The plane did not leave on time, so we arrived at our destination late.

Practice 5) (p. 68)

1. He is poor; nevertheless, he is very happy.
2. Jane did her best in the swimming competition; consequently, she won the gold medal.
3. We need to leave tonight; otherwise, we'll be late for the meeting.
4. Her mom is good at cooking; similarly, she is good at cooking.

Practice 6) (p. 69)

1. C (Compound)

   The Japanese flag is red and white; moreover / in addition / also /

furthermore, the Canadian flag is red and white.

2. S (Simple)
3. C (Compound)

   The weather is bad; therefore / consequently / as a result, the plane cannot take off on time.
4. S (Simple)

Practice 7) (p. 70)

1. C
2. IC : Some of questions → Some questions / Some of the questions
3. C
4. IC : are → is
5. C

Task 1. (p. 71)

Education: A Reflection of Society

In contrast, the Japanese value education highly. They place such importance on it that most of the students complete not only primary school but also high school. Public schools are all both free and egalitarian; therefore, all students are considered equal, and/for they learn the same material. For social reasons, it's important for a student to receive a university degree and a degree from 'the right university', so all of the students have to go through 'examination hell.' There are difficult exams for entrance to all universities, to many of the better primary and secondary schools and even to some kindergartens! A lot of Japanese students need great discipline. Because of studying, a number of students do not have time for hobbies, nor do they enjoy their social life. Results of these exams affect the entire family, for there is high status or social position for the whole family when the children have high test scores.

(from Baker, L. R. et al. 2003. Interactions 2: Integrated Skills. McGraw-Hill)

Unit 5 Noun Clauses and Adjective Clauses

Test yourself!

Unscramble the sentence. Add the proper punctuation in the end.

(1) ______________________________

(insisted, they, that, dinner, we, have, them, with)

(2) ______________________________

(you, have, found, that, the, keys, lost, you) (Question)

(3) ______________________________

(friend, a, is, who, someone, chats, with, on, you, the, Internet)

(4) ______________________________

(pocket, wearing, jacket, Mary, a, that, has, a, is, blue)

Grammar Tips!

명사절은 문장 안에서 명사의 역할을 하며, 문장의 주어, 보어, 목적어로 쓰인다. 형용사절은 흔히 관계사절이라고도 하는데 바로 앞에 나오는 명사(선행사)를 수식한다. 선행사가 형용사절 내에서 어떤 역할을 하는가에 따라 주격, 목적격, 소유격 관계대명사가 쓰인다.

A. Noun Clauses

A noun is used as a subject or an object in a sentence. A noun clause is also used as a subject or an object. In other words, a noun clause is used in the same way as a noun. Look at the sentences in the following:

Used as a subject	Used as an object
(a) His story was interesting. (b) What he said was interesting.	I heard his story. I heard what he said.

There are a few ways to make noun clauses. In each case, you can use different conjunctions (=connecting words). When you make a noun clause, the word order is conj. + S + V. Look at different types of noun clauses.

1. Noun clauses with 'that'

Statements (Expression of an idea or fact)	Noun clauses
(a) He is a good doctor.	I think (that) he is a good doctor.
(b) The world is round.	That the world is round is a fact. =It is a fact that the world is round.

2. Noun clauses with a question word

Questions	Noun clauses
(a) What happened?	Please tell me what happened.
(b) Who is she?	I don't know who she is.
(c) What did he say?	What he said surprised me.

As seen above, noun clauses can begin with a question word. However, the word order in a noun clause is not the same as the word order in a question. Where does she live? (Question) → I don't know where she lives. (Statement with noun clauses)

3. Noun clauses with 'whether' or 'if'

Yes/No Questions	Noun clauses
(a) Will he come?	I don't know whether he will come. I don't know if he will come.
(b) Does she need help?	I wonder whether she needs help. I wonder if she needs help.

In situations where there is no question word used (a 'yes or no' question), you can use if or whether to begin the noun clause in the sentence.

Grammar Tips!

간접의문문이 명사절로 쓰이는 경우가 있다. 간접의문문이란 의문문의 형태가 문장 내에서 주어, 보어, 목적어가 되는 것으로, 이때 어순에 주의해야 한다. 예를 들어, 직접의문문 What time is it? (몇 시 입니까?)는 간접의문문이 되면, Do you know *what time it is*? (지금 몇 시인지 아십니까?)로 바뀐다. 여기서 주의할 것은 간접의문문의 어순 [의문사+주어+동사]이다. 또 다른 예로, Where does he live? 는 Can you tell me *where he lives*?로 바뀌며, Where did he live?는 Do you know *where he lived*?로 바뀐다. 이때 조동사 do/does/did는 쓰지 않고 시제와 주어의 인칭에 따라 바꾸어야 한다. 하지만 그 외의 조동사는 문장에서 그대로 쓴다. 예를 들어 What can you do?는 Please tell me *what you can do.* 로 바뀐다.

이처럼 의문사가 있는 경우는 [의문사+주어+동사]순이지만, 의문사가 없는 간접의문문의 경우는 의문사를 대신하여 명사절 접속사 [if/whether+주어+동사]순으로 바뀐다. 예를 들어, Will she come?은 I don't know *if/whether she will come.*으로 Does she need help?는 I wonder *if/whether she needs help.*로 쓸 수 있다.

4. Question words followed by 'to infinitive' (to + verb)

(a) I don't know what I should do.
= I don't know what to do.
(b) Please tell me how I can get to the bus station.
= Please tell me how to get to the bus station.

When a noun clause begins with question word + S + can/should + V, the noun clause can be changed to question word + to + verb if the subject in the main clause and noun clause are the same as in sentence (a). This pattern can also be used if the subject in the noun clause 'I' is referring to the object 'me' in the main clause as in sentence (b).

Practice 1) Complete the sentences making the sentence in each parenthesis as a noun clause.

1. (James was an excellent swimmer.)

   I think ______________________________.

2. (What was he talking about?)

   ______________________________ was interesting.

3. (Who are those people?)

   I don't know ______________________________.

4. (Why did they leave the country?)

   ______________________________ is a secret.

Practice 2) Change the noun clauses into 'to infinitive' phrases.

1. I don't know what I should do.

   ____

2. He told me when I should come.

   ____

3. The plumber told me how I could fix the leak in the sink.

   ____

4. Jane told us where we could find it.

____

5. Special usage of noun clauses

(a) I insisted that he pay me the money.
(b) I recommended that she not go to the concert.
(c) I suggested that she see a doctor.
(d) It is important that they be told the truth.

(e) Whoever wants to come is welcome.
=Anyone who wants to come is welcome.
(f) He always says whatever comes into his mind.
=He always says anything that comes into his mind.

As you see in (a) to (d), we use a base form verb (동사원형) when the following verbs are used as the main verbs: **insist, recommend, suggest, demand, request, advise, ask, propose**. This pattern is also used with some adjectives: **it is important (that), it is necessary (that), it is essential (that), it is vital (that).**

In addition, relative clause markers (who, whom, which, where, when, what) + ever are used as a connector with the meaning of emphasis (~은 무엇이든지).

Grammar Tips!

제안, 주장, 명령, 요구 등의 동사가 '당위성'을 나타낼 때는 명사절 that절 안에는 조동사 should가 쓰인다. 조동사 should는 생략 가능하기 때문에 명사절 안에 동사는 원형을 쓴다. 예를 들어, I insisted that he pay me the money.를 I insisted that he *paid* me the money.(x)로 되면 틀린 문장이 된다.
또한 관계사(who, whom, which, where, when, what)+ever가 명사절(~하는 사람/것은 누구나/무엇이든)의 의미로 쓰인다. 예를 들어, Whoever wants to come is welcome.

=Anyone who wants to come is welcome.은 '오고 싶은 사람은 누구나 환영 받는다'는 뜻이고, He always says whatever comes into his mind. =He always says anything that comes into his mind. '그는 항상 마음에 떠오르는 것은 무엇이든 말한다.'로 해석된다.

Practice 3) Correct the errors in each sentence. Each sentence has one error.

1. I suggest that he takes a vacation.

☞ Correction:

2. He demanded that she apologized to him.

☞ Correction:

3. Her advisor recommended that she takes five courses.

☞ Correction:

4. He insisted that the new baby was named after his grandfather.

☞ Correction:

Practice 4) Complete the following by using '-ever' words (whatever, wherever, whoever).

1. I don't like ________ he says.

2. Do not trust ___________ says that.

3. He is free to go anyplace he wishes. He can go _________ he wants.

4. I don't know what you should do about that problem. Do ________ seems best to you.

B. Adjective clauses with relative pronouns

(a) Crowded holiday resorts are not very pleasant.
(b) Holiday resorts which are crowded are not very pleasant.

The word 'crowded' in sentence (a) is an adjective. In sentence (b), 'which are crowded' is a clause that is doing exactly the same work as the adjective: it is describing the holiday resorts. We call this an adjective clause or a relative clause because it 'relates' to the noun. Relative clauses, like adjectives, can describe persons, things, and events.

We use who in a relative clause when we are talking about people (not things). We use who instead of he/she/they. Instead of who, that can be also used. When we are talking about things, we use that or which (not who) in a relative clause. That is more common than which. The following shows relative pronouns.

Different types of relative pronouns

Precedent(선행사)	Subject	Object	Possessive
People	who	whom	whose
Things	which	which	of which (=whose)
People & Things	that	that	–

1. How to make a relative clause replacing a subject

(a) I met a woman. She can speak English very well. (2 sentences)

→ I met a woman who can speak English very well. (1 sentence)

Look at these two sentences. Which word gives the same information in the two sentences? A woman and she. Therefore, instead of repeating the same information (she), you can combine the two sentences using an appropriate relative clause marker. In this case, 'who' is used because a woman is a person, and also, it comes in place of the subject of the second sentence.

2. How to make a relative clause replacing an object

The man was Mr. Jones. + I saw him.
→ The man whom I saw was Mr. Jones.
→ The man that I saw was Mr. Jones.
→ The man — I saw was Mr. Jones.

3. How to make a relative clause replacing an object of a preposition

She is the woman. + I told you about her.
→ She is the woman about whom I told you.
→ She is the woman whom I told you about.
→ She is the woman that I told you about.
→ She is the woman about that I told you. (x)

The preposition can be placed before or after 'whom'. However, when 'that' is used, the preposition should always come at the end of the sentence.

4. How to make a relative clause replacing a possessive pronoun

The student writes well. + I am reading her composition.
→ The student writes well. + I am reading the student's composition.
whose
→ The student whose composition I am reading writes well.

As you see in the example, 'whose' is used to replace the possessive pronoun 'her'. When you use 'whose', it should be followed by a noun that it belongs to: whose composition.

Practice 5) Combine the two sentences using a proper relative clause marker. Use the second sentence as an adjective clause.

1. I thanked the woman. She helped me.

2. I am using a sentence. It contains an adjective clause.

3. Algebra problems contain letters. They stand for unknown numbers.

4. The people were very nice. We visited them yesterday.

5. Mr. James has a painting. Its value is inestimable.

C. Adjective clauses with relative adverbs

Different types of relative adverbs

Precedent(선행사)	Relative adverb	Preposition + relative pronoun
The place	where	in (at, on) + which
The time	when	in (at, on) + which
The reason	why	for which
The way	how	in which

1. Relative adverb that modifies a place: where

The building is very old. + He lives in that building.
→ The building where he lives is very old.
→ The building in which he lives is very old.
→ The building which he lives in is very old.
→ The building that he lives in is very old.
→ The building that/which he lives – is very old. (X)
→ The building where he lives in is very old. (X)

When an adjective clause modifies a noun that describes a place (city, country, room, house, etc.), the relative adverb 'where' can be used in place of 'preposition + noun'. You can also use 'preposition + relative pronoun' to replace 'where'. Look at the examples above. Do not use a preposition when a relative adverb is used as in the last sentence.

2. Relative adverb that modifies a time expression: when

I will never forget the day. + I met you then (on that day).
→ I will never forget the day when I met you.
→ I will never forget the day on which I met you.
→ I will never forget the day that I met you.

When an adjective clause modifies a noun that describes a specific time (year, day, time, century, etc.), the relative adverb 'when' can be used in place of 'preposition + noun' in the adjective clause. You can also use 'preposition + relative pronoun' to replace 'when'. Instead of 'preposition + relative pronoun', that can be used as you see in the example above.

3. Relative adverb that modifies a reason: why

I don't know the reason. + They came for the reason.
→ I don't know the reason (why) they came.
→ I don't know why they came.
→ I don't know the reason for which they came.

When an adjective clause modifies a noun that describes a specific reason, the relative adverb 'why' can be used in place of 'preposition + noun'. Also 'for which' can replace 'why'.

4. Relative adverb that modifies a way: how

I taught her the way. + She finished the job in the way.
→ She finished the job the way I taught her.
→ She finished the job how I taught her.
→ She finished the job the way how I taught her. (x)

When an adjective clause modifies a noun that describes a specific way, the relative adverb 'how' can be used in place of 'preposition+ noun' in the adjective clause. Also 'in which' can replace 'how'.

Grammar Tips!

관계부사, where, when, why가 쓰인 관계부사절에서는 [선행사+관계사, 선행사+(관계사 생략), (선행사 생략)+관계사]로 표현할 수 있으나, 관계부사 how는 항상 선행사 the way 나 관계부사 how만 쓰지, the way how로 같이 쓰지 않는다.

Practice 6) Combine the two sentences. Use the second sentence as an adjective clause using a relative adverb.

1. I live in a dormitory. Students from many different countries live in the dormitory.

 ______________________________

2. July is the month. The weather is usually the hottest then (in that month).

➡ ______________________________

3. That is the way. It happened (in the way).

➡ ______________________________

4. Please tell me the reason. You majored in history (for the reason).

➡ ______________________________

Practice 7) Translate the following sentences into English using clue words given in the parenthesis.

1. 테이블 위에 있는 그 책은 내 것이다. (book, on, mine)

2. 어제 밤에 우리가 봤던 영화는 아주 좋지는 않았다. (movie, we, see, last night, very)

3. 내가 얘기했던 그 여자가 저쪽에 서 있다. (woman, tell, about, standing, over there)

4. 1950년대는 의사들이 왕진을 했던 때이다. (1950s, time, make, doctors, house calls)

4. Two usages of relative clauses

There are two kinds of relative clauses: essential (제한적 용법) and non-essential (계속적 용법). For essential relative clauses, **you do not use commas** because they provide essential (=important) information about the nouns they modify. On the other hand, for non-essential relative clauses, **you use commas** because they provide additional information about the nouns they modify.

(a) We took some children on a picnic. **The children *who* wanted to play soccer** ran to the open field as soon as we arrived at the park. The others played a different game.	→ No comma here means that only some of the children wanted to play soccer. The adjective clause is used to identify which children wanted to play soccer and therefore, ran to the open field.
(b) We took some children on a picnic. **The children, *who* wanted to play soccer**, ran to the open field as soon as we arrived at the park.	→ The use of commas means that all of the children wanted to play soccer and all of the children ran to an open field. The adjective clause is used only to give additional information about the children.

Practice 8) Combine the two sentences using a relative clause. Add a comma if necessary.

1. The woman is a doctor. She lives next door.

2. My brother Jim is a doctor. He lives in Houston.

3. Ann is very friendly. She lives next door.

Unit in a Nutshell

- **Noun clauses** function as a noun in a sentence (subject, object, complement) and **adjective clauses** function as an adjective in a sentence modifying a noun.
- An adjective clause, or a **relative clause**, modifies a noun that precedes the relative clause, and the **subjective relative pronoun** changes depending on the type of noun it modifies (persons ➡ who, that; things ➡ that, which).
- An **objective relative pronoun** is used if the modified noun is the object in the relative clause (persons ➡ who(m), that; things ➡ which, that), and it can be omitted.
- A **relative adverb** is used in place of 'prep + relative pronoun' when the precedent (선행사) describes place (where), time (when), way (how), or reason (why).

Practice 9) Correct or Incorrect?

Read the following sentences. If it is correct, circle C. If it is not correct, circle IC. If you circle IC, correct the mistake.

1. He recommended that she attended the workshop. (C IC)

   ☞ Correction:

2. Can you tell me what anybody saw you? (C IC)

   ☞ Correction:

3. That is the village in that he lives. (C IC)

   ☞ Correction:

4. According to the doctrine of utilitarianism, which brings about happiness has utility. (C IC)

   ☞ Correction:

5. It is vital that no one else know about the secret government operation. (C IC)

   ☞ Correction:

6. There is great progress in the medical field where discoveries are made every day. (C IC)

   ☞ Correction:

Writing in Action

Task 1.

Complete the following story by filling in the blanks with the correct relative clause markers.

A Word with Many Meanings

For the French, friendship is a one-to-one relationship ________ demands keen awareness of the other person's intellect, temperament, and particular interests. A friend is someone ________ brings out your own best qualities. [...] For Germans, ________ friendships are based on mutuality of feeling, deep disagreement on any subject ________ matters to both is [...] a tragedy.

Germans form friendships early in life, and friends usually become part of each other's family life. As a result, Mead reports, young Germans __________ come to the United States often have difficulty making friends with Americans, ___________ friendships are less permanent.

British friendships, __________ usually remain outside the family, follow yet another pattern. According to Mead, shared activity is the basis for friendship among the British. British friends may not be as deeply attached to each other as German friends, but their relationships can survive a long separation.

(from Marjorie Fuchs and Margaret Bonner. 2000. Focus on Grammar. Longman.)

Task 2.

Write one or two paragraphs about your favorite movie or actor/actress. Use noun clauses and adjective clauses you have learned in this unit. Before writing the paragraphs, think about the following questions.

Choose one.

(1) What is your favorite movie? What is it about? Why do you like it? Write the story in detail.

(2) Who is your favorite actor/actress? Why do you like the actor or actress? Describe the person in detail.

Unit 5 Answer Key

Test yourself! (p. 77)

(1) They insisted that we have dinner with them.

(2) Have you found the keys that you lost?

(3) A friend is someone who chats with you on the Internet.

(4) Mary is wearing a blue jacket that has a pocket.

Practice 1) (p. 81)

1. I think that James was an excellent swimmer.
2. What he was talking about was interesting.
3. I don't know who those people are.
4. Why they left the country is a secret.

Practice 2) (p. 81)

1. I don't know what to do.
2. He told me when to come.
3. The plumber told me how to fix the leak in the sink.
4. Jane told us where to find it.

Practice 3) (p. 83)

1. I suggest that he take a vacation.
2. He demanded that she apologize to him.
3. Her advisor recommended that she take five courses.
4. He insisted that the new baby be named after his grandfather.

Practice 4) (p. 83)

1. I don't like whatever he says.
2. Do not trust whoever says that.
3. He is free to go anyplace he wishes. He can go wherever he wants.
4. I don't know what you should do about that problem. Do whatever seems best to you.

Practice 5) (p. 86)

1. I thanked the woman who/that helped me.
2. I am using a sentence which/that contains an adjective clause.
3. Algebra problems contain letters which/that stand for unknown numbers.
4. The people whom/that we visited yesterday were very nice.
5. Mr. James has a painting whose value is inestimable.

Practice 6) (p. 89)

1. I live in a dormitory where students from many different countries live.
2. July is the month when the weather is usually the hottest.
3. That is how it happened./That is the way it happened.
4. Please tell me the reason why you majored in history.

Practice 7) (p. 90)

1. The book that/which is on the table is mine.
2. The movie which/that we saw last night was not very good.
3. The woman whom I told you about is standing over there.

4. The 1950s was the time when doctors made house calls.

Practice 8) (p. 92)

1. The woman who lives next door is a doctor.(No comma)
2. My brother Jim, who lives in Houston, is a doctor.
3. Ann, who lives next door, is very friendly.

Practice 9) (p. 93)

1. IC : attended → attend
2. IC : what → whether/if
3. IC : in that → in which/where
4. IC : which → whatever
5. C
6. C

Task 1. (p. 94)

A Word with Many Meanings

For the French, friendship is a one-to-one relationship that/which demands keen awareness of the other person's intellect, temperament, and particular interests. A friend is someone who/that brings out your own best qualities. [...] For Germans, whose friendships are based on mutuality of feeling, deep disagreement on any subject that/which matters to both is [...] a tragedy.

Germans form friendships early in life, and friends usually become part of each other's family life. As a result, Mead reports, young Germans who/that come to the United States often have difficulty making friends with Americans, whose friendships are less permanent.

British friendships, which usually remain outside the family, follow yet another pattern. According to Mead, shared activity is the basis for friendship among the British. British friends may not be as deeply attached to each other as German friends, but their relationships can survive a long separation.

(from Marjorie Fuchs and Margaret Bonner. 2000. Focus on Grammar. Longman.)

marcher ne jamai
入試

Unit 6 Adverbial Clauses

Test yourself!

Fill in the blank with a proper connector.

________ I go home for the summer, I like to spend a lot of time with my family at my parent's house. I have to wear a lot of sunscreen ________ I protect my skin from the sun. We play ________ it is dark outside. ________ I am tired at the end of each day, I am happy ________ I have had so much fun.

Grammar Tips!

영어에서 접속사 (conjunction)의 역할은 단어와 단어, 구와 구 그리고 절과 절을 연결하는 것이다. 시간, 이유, 때 등의 의미를 전달하는 부사절을 만들기 위해 다양한 접속사를 사용하는데, 이때 접속사는 부사절의 맨 앞에 온다는 것을 기억하자. 예를 들면 He was absent because she was sick. (그는 그녀가 아파서 오지 못했다) 와 Because he was absent, she was sick. (그가 오지 못해서 그녀는 아팠다.) 이 두 문장을 보면 이유의 접속사 because 를 어디에 붙이는가에 따라 문장의 의미가 전혀 달라짐을 볼 수 있다. 따라서 두 개의 절 혹은 문장을 연결할 때 이유나 조건 때에 해당하는 부분이 어디인가 확인하고 그 앞에 접속사를 붙여야 한다.

A. Definitions of IC (independent clause) and DC (dependent clause)

Independent Clause: An independent clause must include a subject and verb. An independent clause also expresses a complete thought and can stand alone as a sentence. For example, 'I go to the store on Sundays', expresses a complete thought, and therefore, this can stand alone (=independent clause) as a sentence.

Dependent Clause: A dependent clause also includes a subject and a verb. However, a dependent clause does not express a complete thought, and therefore cannot stand alone as a sentence. For example, 'When I go to the store on Sundays.' This is not a complete thought, so it cannot stand alone (=dependent clause). To make it a complete sentence we must add an independent clause: When I go to the store on Sundays, I always buy milk.

This unit will be focusing on adverbial dependent clauses, which begin with a subordinating conjunction(종속접속사). Some common subordinating conjunctions include: after, before, when, since, until, while, because, as, in order that, although, though, even though, whereas, if, unless, as if, only if, even if, whether, in case (that).

1. Combining Dependent and Independent Clauses: Avoiding Fragment Sentences

(a) Because she likes to swim. -- Fragment
DEPENDENT CLAUSE

(b) Because she likes to swim, she often goes to the pool. -- Complete Sentence
DEPENDENT CLAUSE　INDEPENDENT CLAUSE

(c) She loves the ocean because she likes to swim. -- Complete Sentence
INDEPENDENT CLAUSE　DEPENDENT CLAUSE

A dependent clause cannot stand alone, and it does not express a complete thought. Therefore, it cannot be a sentence. If a dependent clause is used like a sentence, it is an example of a **fragment**, or incomplete sentence. To make a dependent clause a complete sentence, it must be combined with an independent clause. For example, sentence (a) is incorrect because it is a fragment. We need to know what she does because she likes to swim. In sentences (b) and (c), we include an **independent clause** making them complete sentences. Notice that in sentence (b) we use a comma, and in sentence (c) we do not. In sentence (b), the dependent clause comes first, so we need a comma. However, in sentence (c) the dependent clause follows the independent clause, so we do not need a comma. This rule always holds true, except when using 'while' and 'whereas' to express a contrast. Compare the following sentences.

(a) She likes ice cream, while he prefers potato chips.
(b) My phone rang while I was sleeping.

In sentence (a) 'while' indicates a difference or contrast. Therefore, we need a comma (,) even though the dependent clause is not first. On the other hand, 'while' in sentence (b) tells us when the independent clause happened. If 'while' is used to indicate time, it does not need a comma when the dependent clause follows the independent clause.

Grammar Tips!

영어에서 주절 (independent clause)과 종속절 (dependent clause)을 써서 하나의 문장을 만드는 경우 주절이 앞에 오면 쉼표 (comma)를 사용하지 않지만 종속절이 앞에 올 경우에는 쉼표를 주절 앞에 붙여 준다. 하지만 예외가 있는데 반대의 의미를 나타내는 while, whereas (--한 반면에)의 경우, 종속절이 뒤에 오는 경우에도 그 앞에 comma를 붙여준다.

2. Forming questions with dependent and independent clauses

(a) When you eat ice cream quickly, do you get a headache?
(b) Do you get a headache when you eat ice cream quickly?

In making a question using a dependent and independent clause, notice that the use of the comma is the same with questions as it is with statements. The dependent clause has not changed. The question is asked only in the independent clause 'do you get a headache', leaving the dependent clause the same.

Practice 1) Add a comma where it is necessary.

1. They go to the movies when they are bored.

2. Though I enjoy skiing I did not go to the mountains this winter.

3. Did the team celebrate after they won the game?

4. Unless I'm prepared for a test I won't sleep well the night before.

5. In order that he may win the contest he practices every night.

6. If it is on Friday will you come to my party?

Practice 2) Read the following sentences. Write FRAGMENT next to those that are not complete. Write CORRECT next to those that are complete.

1. Unless she comes to my house. ____________________

2. Do you like to eat lemons even though they are sour? ____________________

3. Because she is very beautiful and kind. ____________________

4. Whenever I drink coffee, I get lots of energy. ____________________

5. I will work until the project is finished. ____________________

B. Types of adverbial clauses and subordinating conjunctions

Adverbial clauses, a type of dependent clause, are used to give more information about what happens in the independent clause. An adverbial clause begins with a subordinating conjunction (종속 접속사). There are four basic types of adverbial clauses and subordinating conjunctions: time, cause and purpose, opposition, and condition.

Time: after, before, while, since, until, when, as
Cause and Effect: since, as, in order that, so that, because
Opposition: though, although, even though, while, whereas
Condition: if, unless, only if, whether, even if, in case (that)

1. Using adverbial clauses to show 'time'

(a) When I was a child, I liked to read mystery novels.
(b) She brushed her teeth before she washed her face.
(c) Until my mom wakes me, I will sleep.

An adverbial clause can tell us when the action in the independent clause occurred or will occur.

● General verb rules for time subordinating conjunctions

Subordinating Conjunction	Time Reference	Dependent Clause Verb Tense	Independent Clause Verb Tense
When	Future	Present/Present Continuous	Future/Future Continuous
	Continual	Present/Present Continuous	Present (Present Continuous)*
	Past	Past/Past Continuous	Past/Past Continuous
	Future	When I feel tired, I will go to bed.	
	Continual	When he reads books, he likes to sit in his favorite chair.	
	Past	I was watching TV when I heard the phone ring.	

Before/After	Future Continual Past	Present Present Past/Past Continuous	Future Present Past/Past Continuous
	Future Continual Past	Before I visit my brother, I will visit my sister. After I eat dinner, I always drink coffee. I brushed my teeth before I went to bed.	
Until	Future Continual Past	Present Present Past/(Past Continuous)*	Future Present Past/(Past Continuous)*
	Future Continual Past	Until the game starts, I will rest. I always go running until my legs start to hurt. I studied until my eyes could not stay open.	
Since	Past	Past	Present Perfect/(Past Perfect)*
	Past	I have studied Japanese since I was six.	
While/As	Future Continual Past	Present Continuous Present/Present Continuous Past/Past Continuous	Future/Future Continuous Present/Present Continuous Past/Past Continuous
	Future Continual Past	While he is biking, his friends will be running. She always snores while she is sleeping. As I was combing my hair, I found a gray hair on my head.	

* All examples in parenthesis are possible, but not as common.

Grammar Tips!

시간을 나타내는 종속 접속사를 사용할 경우, 종속절은 미래 시제 대신에 현재시제를 사용한다. 즉 When he arrives, Susan will go home. (그가 도착하면 수잔은 집에 갈 것이다) 라고 할 때 비록 아직 그가 도착을 하지 않은 미래의 시간을 이야기하지만 When he will arrive 라고 하지 않고 When he arrives 라는 현재형을 사용한다. 또 since 라는 종속 접속사를 사용할 경우 since 절은 과거시제를 사용하고, 주절은 현재 완료형 시제를 사용해서 (--때부터 계속 -하다) 라는 구문을 만든다. 예를 들어 I have lived in Hawaii since I was five. (나는 다섯살 때부터 하와이에서 살았다.)

Practice 3) Use an appropriate time subordinating conjunction to complete the sentence.

1. ________________ I went to the store, I visited my grandmother.

2. I have loved cats ________________ I was young.

3. I will stay at your house ________________ the work is done.

4. ________________ I am studying, my friends will be eating dinner.

2. Using adverbial clauses to show 'cause and effect'

(a) As he is a key member of our team, he will work hard to help us win.
(b) She will eat lots of vegetables in order that she (may) have a healthy diet.
(c) Since I received all As in my classes, I will receive a scholarship.
(d) He is working out so that he stays in shape.

An adverbial clause can tell us why the action in the independent clause occurred or will occur. Note that 'as', 'because', and 'since' all mean the same thing when they are used as a subordinating conjunction to express cause and effect. 'In order that' and 'so that' tell the purpose of an action and are both used in the same manner, except 'in order that' is followed by a subjunctive verb (동사의 원형). Note that in sentence (b), the verb following 'in order that' takes the subjunctive form. However, the verb following 'so that' in sentence (d), you can use either a simple present tense or subjunctive verb form.

Practice 4) Use an appropriate cause and effect subordinating conjunction to complete the sentence.

1. ________________ I want to see you, I will go to the library.

2. I will fly to America ________________ I may see my best friend.

3. I practiced hard every day ________________ I wanted to win.

3. Using adverbial clauses to show 'opposition'

(a) I studied all day for the test even though I don't like studying.
(b) I prefer to watch tennis, whereas they like hockey.
(c) Although she doesn't like dogs, her family will buy a dog tomorrow.

An adverbial clause can show us something in opposition to what happened or will happen in the independent clause. Note that 'even though', 'though', and 'although' mean the same thing. Also, 'whereas' and 'while' mean the same thing when functioning as opposition subordinating conjunctions. As in sentence (b), 'whereas' and 'while' always use a comma when expressing opposition even if the dependent clause is second. This is an exception to the standard rule.

Practice 5) Use an appropriate opposition subordinating conjunction to complete the sentence.

1. ________________ I miss my family, I am happy that I am studying abroad.

2. She is very talkative and fun, ________________ her brother is rather boring.

3. The bird was not hurt ________________ it flew into a window.

4. Using adverbial clauses to show 'condition'

(a) I will go to the party only if you promise to talk to me the entire time.
(b) Unless you sing her a lullaby and read her a book, she will not fall asleep.
(c) I have a backup computer we can use in case your computer dies.

An adverbial clause can be used to show under what condition(s) the independent clause happened or will happen. Some of the most common condition subordinating conjunctions include: if, unless, only if, whether, even if, and in case (that).

Practice 6) Use an appropriate condition subordinating conjunction to complete the sentence.

1. I will miss you ________________ we talk on the phone every day.

2. You should have a backup plan ________________ something goes wrong.

3. ________________ you see my mother, tell her I will be home late.

Unit in a Nutshell

- A dependent clause (DC) does not express a complete thought and cannot stand alone. When a dependent clause is used as a sentence, it is called a fragment or an incomplete sentence.
- When an independent clause (IC) comes first, you don't need to add a comma before the DC. However, when a DC comes first, you need to add a comma before the IC.
- To make an adverbial clause, a subordinating conjunction needs to come before a DC and it expresses time, cause and effect, opposition, or condition.

Practice 7) Correct or Incorrect?

If the sentence is correct, simply write CORRECT. If it is incorrect, rewrite the sentence. If the sentence is a fragment, be creative and complete the sentence with your own words.

1. When I am in the country I love to look at the stars at night. (C IC)
   ☞ Correction:

2. I am scared of dogs I was bit by one last year. (C IC)
   ☞ Correction:

3. They did very well on their test they did not study hard. (C IC)

☞ Correction:

4. Do you like to listen to music while you are studying? (C IC)

☞ Correction:

5. Because it was raining so hard. (C IC)

☞ Correction:

6. I like to walk to school, unless it is raining. (C IC)

☞ Correction:

7. I study very hard I will not pass my class. (C IC)

☞ Correction:

8. Will you visit me while I am working? (C IC)

☞ Correction:

Writing in Action

Task 1.

You are given a dependent clause and an independent clause in each question. Use an appropriate subordinating conjunction and combine the two clauses to form one sentence.

Example: Dependent Clause ➲ I enjoy art.
Independent Clause ➲ I like to visit museums.
Answer: I like to visit museums **because** I enjoy art.

1. Dependent Clause ➲ My cousin likes big dogs.
   Independent Clause ➲ My sister likes small dogs.

   ____

2. Dependent Clause ➲ There is a blizzard.
   Independent Clause ➲ The nurse will have to go to work at the hospital.

   ____

3. Dependent Clause ➲ They are the best team in the world.
   Independent Clause ➲ My favorite team is Manchester United.

   ____

4. Dependent Clause ➡ I was a small child.
Independent Clause ➡ I have studied English.

___

5. Dependent Clause ➡ I have a test I must study for.
Independent Clause ➡ I will come to your party.

___

6. Dependent Clause ➡ The day of the test arrived.
Independent Clause ➡ He never stopped studying.

___

Task 2.
The Happiest Moment of My Life: Writing a Story

When was the happiest moment of your life? What happened? Think about the happiest event or time in your life and write a story about it. When you write, include at least six sentences with dependent clauses using subordinating conjunctions expressing time, cause and effect, opposition, or condition.

To generate ideas for the writing, ask yourself the following questions.

(1) When was the happiest moment in your life?
(2) What happened at that time? Who was involved in the event?
(3) Why did you feel so happy? Why is it so special to you?
(4) What did you learn from this experience?

The Happiest Moment of My Life

Unit 6 Answer Key

Test yourself! (p. 101)

When I go home for the summer, I like to spend a lot of time with my family at my parent's house. I have to wear a lot of sunscreen so that/in order that I protect my skin from the sun. We play until it is dark outside. Although/Even though/Though I am tired at the end of each day, I am happy as/because/since I have had so much fun.

Practice 1) (p. 104)

1. They go to the movies when they are bored. (No Comma)
2. Though I enjoy skiing, I did not go to the mountains this winter.
3. Did the team celebrate after they won the game? (No Comma)
4. Unless I'm prepared for a test, I won't sleep well the night before.
5. In order that he may win the contest, he practices every night.
6. If it is on Friday, will you come to my party?

Practice 2) (p. 105)

1. Fragment
2. Correct
3. Fragment
4. Correct
5. Correct

Practice 3) (p. 108)

1. After/Before I went to the store, I visited my grandmother.

2. I have loved cats since I was young.
3. I will stay at your house until the work is done.
4. While/As/When I am studying, my friends will be eating dinner.

Practice 4) (p. 109)

1. As/Because/Since I want to see you, I will go to the library.
2. I will fly to America in order that/so that I may see my best friend.
3. I practiced hard every day as/because/since I wanted to win.

Practice 5) (p. 110)

1. Even though/Although/Though I miss my family, I am happy that I am studying abroad.
2. She is very talkative and fun, whereas/while her brother is rather boring.
3. The bird was not hurt even though/although/though it flew into a window.

Practice 6) (p. 110)

1. I will miss you even if/unless we talk on the phone every day.
2. You should have a backup plan in case something goes wrong.
3. If you see my mother, tell her I will be home late.

Practice 7) (p. 111)

1. IC : When I am in the country, I love to look at the stars at night.
2. IC : I am scared of dogs since/because/as I was bit by one last year.
3. IC : They did very well on their test even though/although/though

they did not study hard.

4. C
5. IC : Because it was raining so hard, water started to come in the house.
6. IC : I like to walk to school unless it is raining.(No comma)
7. IC : Even if/Unless I study very hard, I will not pass my class.
8. C

Task 1. (p.113)

1. Whereas/while my cousin likes big dogs, my sister likes small dogs.

2. The nurse will have to go work at the hospital even if/whether or not there is a blizzard.

3. My favorite team is Manchester United because/since/as they are the best team in the world.

4. Since I was a small child, I have studied English.

5. Unless/Even though/Although/Though I have a test I must study for, I will come to your party.

6. Until the day of the test arrived, he never stopped studying.

Unit 7 If Clauses and Verbs

Test yourself!

Complete the sentences with proper words and expressions.

(1) What ______________ I do if I won a million dollars?

(2) If I ________________________ a millionaire when the earthquake hit in Haiti, I would have sent a lot of money to help the victims.

(3) If I _____________ a family, I will want to have a nice house.

(4) I would buy the nice car if I _______________ enough money.

Grammar Tips!

영어의 가정법 표현은 일반적으로 사실이 아닌 어떤 상태를 가정해서 이야기 할 때 쓰인다. 따라서 시제를 사용할 때도 과거사실의 반대를 표현하기 위해서는 if 절에 과거완료(had+pp) 시제를, 현재사실의 반대를 표현할 때는 과거시제를 사용하며 주절의 동사는 조동사 would (could/should/might) 를 포함시킨다.

A. Zero Conditional with If Clause

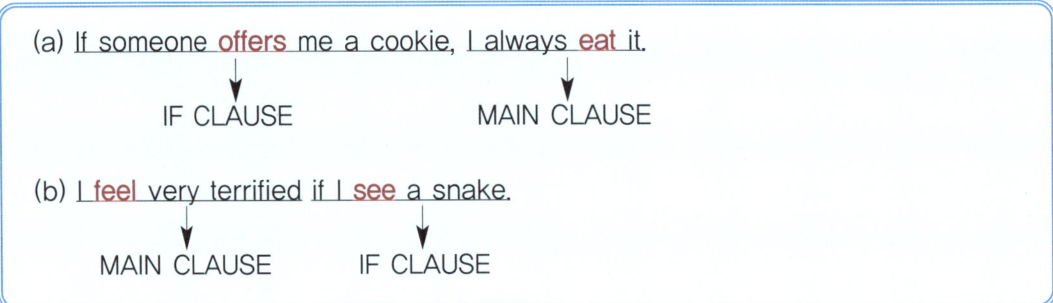

Some conditional sentences state situations that are always true. This type of 'if clause' sentence is called Zero Conditional, and it always uses the simple present tense in both the 'if clause' and the main clause. In the examples of (a) and (b), the speaker always accepts a cookie when it is offered to her, and she is always scared when she sees a snake.

1. How to make affirmative statements in Zero Conditional sentences

(a) If I cook dinner, I always make chicken.
(b) If he has a treat, he shares it with his sister.

2. How to make negative statements in Zero Conditional sentences

(If) + S + do/does not + base form	(If) + S + be (simple present) + not
(a) If he likes a girl, he does not hide it.	(c) She cries for hours if she is not happy.
(b) I watch TV all night long if I do not want to fall asleep.	(d) If the weather is not good, there isn't practice.

Notice that there can be a negative statement in both the 'if clause' and the main clause, and the negative statement is formed the same way in each.

3. How to make questions with Zero Conditional sentences

If + S + simple present verb, do/does + S + base form?	If + S + simple present verb, be (simple present) + S?
(a) If you like a dish, do you eat it often? Yes, I do. / No, I don't. (b) Does he always spend a lot of money if he is on a date? Yes, he does. / No, he doesn't.	(c) If all of his students come to class on time, is Dr. Smith happy? Yes, he is. / No, he isn't. (d) Are you tired if you don't get eight hours of sleep? Yes, I am. / No, I'm not.

Notice that the question is formed in the main clause, and the 'if clause' remains a statement. Also, note in sentences (b) and (d) that the 'if clause' follows the main clause, so you do not need a comma.

Practice 1) Complete the sentences with the proper verb form to create a Zero Conditional. If you see a (+), make an affirmative statement. If you see a (–), make a negative statement.

Ex: If her ________________ , ________________ the phone.
(ex–boyfriend, call, + / she, answer, –)
➲ If her ex–boyfriend calls, she does not answer the phone.

1. If ________________ for more than an hour, ________________ asleep.

(she, read, + / she, fall, +)

2. ________________ to swim if ________________ warm outside?

(he, like, + / it, be, +)

3. If ________________ a test, ________________ well.

(I, have, + / I, sleep, −)

4. If ________________ to study, ________________ his books home.

(he, want, − / he, bring, −)

5. ________________ unhappy if her ________________ near?

(she, be, + / family, be, −)

B. Type 1 Conditional

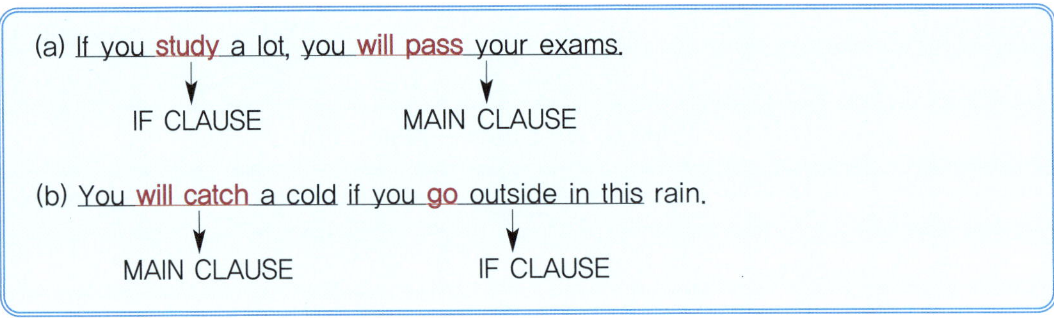

These conditional sentences refer to the present or future and refer to something that is possible. This is called Type 1 Conditional, and it talks about a possible condition in the 'if clause' with a probable result in the main clause. To form a Type 1 Conditional sentence, use the simple present tense for the 'if clause' and simple future for the main clause.

1. How to make affirmative statements in Type 1 Conditional sentences

If + S + simple present, S + simple future
S + simple future + if + S + simple present

(a) If I work for ten hours, she will pay me $200.
(b) The children will be tired if they play all day.

2. How to make negative statements in Type 1 Conditional sentences*

If + S + simple present, S + will + not + base form
S + will + not + base form + if + S + simple present

(a) If I am bored, I will not pay attention.
(b) I will not be sad if she does not come to my birthday party.

*The 'if clause' uses a simple present tense verb. Please refer to the Zero Conditional explanation to see how to make a negative statement in the 'if clause' when using simple present tense.

3. How to make questions with Type 1 Conditional sentences

If + S + simple present, will + S + base form?
Will + S + base form + if + S + simple present?

(a) If I make dinner, will you come to my house to eat?
Yes, I will. / No, I won't (come to your house).
(b) Will they be happy if Spain wins the World Cup?
Yes, they will. / No, they won't (be happy).

Notice that the question is formed in the main clause, and the 'if clause' remains as a statement.

Practice 2) Complete the following sentences with the proper verb form to make Type 1 Conditional sentences. If you see a (+), make an affirmative statement, and if you see a (–), make a negative statement.

Ex: If her ________________ , ________________ the phone. (ex–boyfriend, call, + / she, answer, –)
➡ If her ex–boyfriend calls, she will not answer the phone.

1. If ______________ tired tonight, ______________ with you to the movie.
(I, be, – / I, go, +)

2. ______________ to swim in the race if ______________ his homework?
(he, be able, + / he, finish, –)

3. ______________ tennis on Friday if ______________ too cold.
(I, play, – / the weather, be, +)

C. Type 2 Conditional

(a) If I **were** a billionaire, I **would own** a home on every continent.

IF CLAUSE — MAIN CLAUSE

(b) I **would cry** tears of joy if I **were** able to finish a marathon.

MAIN CLAUSE — IF CLAUSE

Type 2 Conditional refers to the present or future. However, this type of conditional refers to something that is impossible, improbable, or imaginary. The 'if clause' refers to something that is unlikely to happen or a hypothetical situation, and the main clause refers to the probable result. In a Type 2 Conditional sentence, the main clause uses 'would + simple form verb', and the 'if clause' uses the past subjunctive. (The past subjunctive is the same as simple past, except for the past tense of 'be.')

Grammar Tips!

현재사실의 반대를 나타내는 가정법 과거에서는 if 절에 동사의 과거형을 쓴다.
이때 be의 동사의 경우 주어가 1인칭이거나 (I) 3인칭이라 해도 (she/he/it), be동사는 모두 were 의 형태로 쓴다. 예를 들어 If I were able to dance like Michael Jackson, I would be very popular at clubs. (내가 마이클 잭슨처럼 춤을 춘다면 난 클럽에서 매우 인기가 높을 텐데 -->사실은 춤을 그렇게 추지 못함을 의미)

1. How to make affirmative statements in Type 2 Conditional sentences

If + S + past subjunctive, S + would + simple form verb
S + would + simple form verb + if + S + past subjunctive

(a) I would choose to fly if I could have a super hero power.
(b) If the Beatles were all alive, he would pay a $10,000 to see their concert.

2. How to make negative statements in the IC of Type 2 Conditional sentences

If clause, S + would + not + base form

(a) If I had one million dollars, I would not give you any.
(b) Your team would not win if Park Ji-sung played on my soccer team.

3. How to make negative statements in the 'if clause' of Type 2 Conditional sentences

If + S + did not + base form, IC	If + S + were + not, IC
(a) If I did not have a family, I would be very lonely. (b) The Disney Corporation would not exist if children did not like Mickey Mouse.	(c) If she were not happy, she would not stay at her job. (d) I would eat pizza everyday if it were not so unhealthy.

4. How to make questions with Type 2 Conditional sentences

Would + S + base form + if + S + past subjunctive verb?
(a) What would you do if I stole your favorite shirt? (b) If I ran for President of the United States, would you vote for me?

Notice that the question is formed in the main clause and the 'if clause' remains as a statement.

Practice 3) Complete the following sentences with the proper verb form to make Type 2 Conditional sentences. If you see a (+), make an affirmative statement, and if you see a (–), make a negative statement.

Ex: If ________________ her for advice, ________________ the phone.
(President Lee, call, + / she, answer, –)
➡ If President Lee called her for advice, she would not answer the phone.

1. If ______________ your mother, ______________ you to go home and study. (I, be, + / I, tell +)

2. How ______________ if ______________ an Olympic gold medal? (you, feel + / you win +)

3. If ______________ wings, ______________ ever again. (I, have, + / I, walk, −)

4. ______________ on this team if ______________ me? (you, play, + / you, know, −)

D. Type 3 Conditional

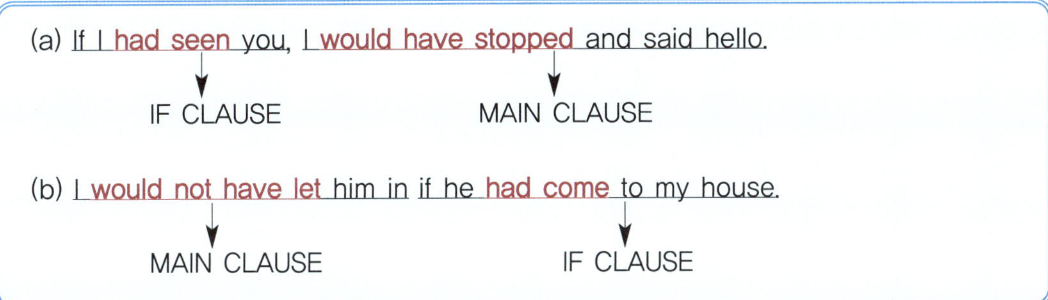

The last type of conditional sentences is Type 3 Conditional. Type 3 Conditional sentences are used to discuss past situations that did not happen and what the result would have been if they did happen. They are constructed with the past perfect (had + past participle) in the 'if clause', and the conditional form (would + have + past participle) in the main clause.

1. How to make affirmative statements in Type 3 Conditional sentences

If + S + had + pp, S + would + have + pp
S + would + have + pp + if + S + had + pp

(a) If I had cooked dinner, you would have complained it was too bland.
(b) If you had watched the game, you would have jumped for joy.
(c) You would have seen my performance if you had gone to the park.
(d) I would have left the door open if I had known you were coming.

2. How to make negative statements in Type 3 Conditional sentences

If + S + had + not + pp, S + would + not + have + pp

(a) If I had not eaten the chicken, I would not have felt sick yesterday.
(b) He would have met you at the park if he had not been busy at home.
(c) He would not have been late to class if the bus had arrived on time.

3. How to make questions with Type 3 Conditional sentences

Would + S + have + pp + if + S + had + pp?
If + S + had + pp, would + S + have + pp?

(a) How would you have gotten to work if your car had not started?
(b) If they had run to class, would they have been on time?

Notice that the question is formed in the main clause and the 'if clause' remains as a statement.

Grammar Tips!

가정법 과거완료는 과거사실에 대한 반대 및 가정을 표현할 때 쓰인다. 즉 -했더라면 -했을 텐데 (결과적으로 -하지 못해서-못했다) 라는 의미를 갖는다. 여기서 한가지 기억할 것은 be able to (=can) 즉 '-할 수 있다' 는 의미의 동사구가 if 절에 사용 될 경우 had been able to + simple verb 대신 could have + past participle를 쓸 수 있고 또 주절에서 사용된 would have been able to + simple verb도 could have + past participle 바꿀 수 있다. 예를 들어 보면 If I had been able to call you, I would have called to apologize. = If I **could have called** you, I would have called to apologize. (내가 너에게 전화를 걸 수 있었더라면, 네게 사과하기 위해 전화를 했을 텐데 - 결국 못했다는 의미를 포함) 또 다른 예는 I **would have been able to call** you if I had had my phone. = I **could have called** you if had had my phone. (내가 전화기를 갖고 있었더라면 네게 전화를 할 수 있었을 텐데-전화기가 없어서 전화를 못했음을 나타냄)

Practice 4) Complete the following sentences with the proper verb form to make Type 3 Conditional sentences. If you see a (+), make an affirmative statement, and if you see a (–), make a negative statement.

Ex: If her ________________ , ________________ the phone.
(ex-boyfriend, call, + / she, answer, –)
➲ If her ex-boyfriend had called, she would not have answered the phone.

1. If ________________ to the store, ________________ enough food.
(he, go, – / we, have, –)

2. If ________________ the book first, ________________ the movie?
(you, read, + / you, see, +)

3. ________________ it was going to rain if ________________ the weather.

(they, know, + / they check +)

Unit in a Nutshell

- Zero Conditional sentences are conditional statements that are always or continually true.
- Type 1 Conditional sentences happen in the present or future and are likely to happen.
- Type 2 Conditional sentences also happen in the present or future but are more unlikely to happen or even impossible or imaginary.
- Type 3 Conditional sentences are something that did not happen in the past and describe what the outcome would have been if they did happen.

Practice 5) Correct or Incorrect?

Read the given circumstance first. Then if the sentence is correct, circle C. If it is incorrect, circle IC and rewrite the correct sentence and identify the type of conditional (zero, 1, 2, or 3).

Example

Circumstance: You often host barbecues at your house and invite your friends. You are speaking to your friend:

1. If I had had a barbeque next week, would you have come? (C IC)
   Correction: If I have a barbeque next week, will you come? (type 1)

 # Circumstance: Yesterday, your friend was in a race, but he couldn' t finish because he was too tired.

1. If he had run every day this month, he would finish the race. (C IC)

☞ Correction:

 # Circumstance: Your friend is Kim Yu Na, and she is talking about her next competition.

2. If I land a triple-triple combination, I will win the competition. (C IC)

☞ Correction:

 # Circumstance: You are considering drinking a milkshake, and you are concerned about your habit.

3. If I have a milkshake, I always drink it too fast and get a headache.
(C IC)

☞ Correction:

 # Circumstance: A boy who is terrible at sports talks about being a professional baseball player when he grows up.

4. If I am a professional baseball player, I will play for the New York Yankees.
(C IC)

☞ Correction:

Practice 6) Translate the following sentences into English.

1. 난 친구들이 카페로 불러내면 절대 거절하지 않는다.

2. 그녀는 저 많은 구두들만 사들이지 않았어도 차를 팔지 않아도 되었을 텐데.

3. 내가 만약 왕이라면 난 모든 숙제를 없애 버릴텐데!

4. 내가 만약 네가 가장 좋아하는 쿠키를 만든다면 좀 먹겠니?

Writing in Action

Task 1.

Read the paragraph below and complete the sentences with the appropriate forms of the verbs given in the parenthesis.

The Beach

I love to go to the beach. In the summer, if it _________ sunny, I _________ on my swimsuit, _________ a towel, and _________ to the beach. (be, put, grab, drive) If there _________ a lot of traffic, I _________ frustrated because I am so anxious to see the ocean and smell the salty air. (be, get) Every time I go to the beach I think, 'If I _________ a million dollars, I _________ a house right on the beach, so I would never have to leave'.(have, buy)

The weatherman says it will be sunny and warm tomorrow, so I am planning to go to the beach. When I wake up, if the sky _________ clear, I _________ to East Beach to meet my friends. (be, go) We _________ if the waves _________ big enough. (surf, be) If they ________ small, then we ________ beach volleyball instead. (be, play) We will spend hours and hours in the sun. If we ________ not ______ a lot of sunscreen, we ________ sunburned at the end of the day. (use, be) Whenever this happens, I think 'if I ________ careful, I ________ not ________ so red'. (be, become)

Task 2.

Making a Wish List

Think about 7 things that you want to do now or in the future as well as something you wanted to do but couldn't do in the past. In addition, think about something you don't want to do now or in the future as well as something that you regret doing in the past. In making the wish list, use various types of conditional clauses you learned in this unit.

My Wish List

I. ____

II. ____

III. ____

IV. ____

V. ____

VI. ____

VII. ____

Unit 7 Answer Key

Test yourself! (p. 119)

(1) What would I do if I won a million dollars?

(2) If I had been a millionaire when the earthquake hit in Haiti, I would have sent a lot of money to help the victims.

(3) If I have a family, I will want to have a nice house.

(4) I would buy the nice car if I had enough money.

Practice 1) (p. 121)

1. If she reads for more than an hour, she falls asleep.
2. Does he like to swim if it is warm outside?
3. If I have a test, I do not sleep well.
4. If he doesn't want to study, he doesn't bring his books home.
5. Is she unhappy if her family is not near?

Practice 2) (p. 124)

1. If I am not tired tonight, I will go with you to the movie.
2. Will he be able to swim in the race if he does not finish his homework?
3. I will not play tennis on Friday if the weather is too cold.

Practice 3) (p. 126)

1. If I were your mother, I would tell you to go home and study.
2. How would you feel if you won an Olympic gold medal?
3. If I had wings, I would not walk ever again.

4. Would you play on this team if you did not know me?

Practice 4) (p. 129)

1. If he had not gone to the store, we would not have had enough food.
2. If you had read the book first, would you have seen the movie?
3. They would have known it was going to rain if they had checked the weather.

Practice 5) (p. 130)

1. IC : If he had run every day this month, he would have finished the race. (Type 3)
2. C (Type 1)
3. C (Zero Conditional)
4. IC : If I were a professional baseball player, I would play for the New York Yankees. (Type 2)

Practice 6) (p. 132)

1. I never say no if my friends invite me to a coffee shop/café.
2. If she hadn't bought all of those shoes, she wouldn't have had to sell her car.
3. If I were the king, I would end all homework!
4. Will you eat some if I make your favorite cookies?

Task 1. (p. 132)

The Beach

I love to go to the beach. In the summer, if it **is** sunny, I **put** on my swimsuit, **grab** a towel, and **drive** to the beach. If there **is** a lot of traffic, I **get** frustrated because I am so anxious to see the ocean and smell the salty air. Every time I go to the beach, I think, 'If I **had** a million dollars, I **would buy** a house right on the beach, so I would never have to leave'.

The weatherman says it will be sunny and warm tomorrow, so I am planning to go to the beach. When I wake up, if the sky **is** clear, I **will go** to East Beach to meet my friends. We **will surf** if the waves **are** big enough. If they **are** small, then we **will play** beach volleyball instead. We will spend hours and hours in the sun. If we **do not use** a lot of sunscreen, we **will be** sunburned at the end of the day. Whenever this happens, I think, 'if I **had been** careful, I **would not have become** so red'.

Unit 8 Gerund vs. Infinitive

Test yourself!

Fill in each blank with a proper form of the given verb.

When I got in the café, I found my friend ____________ (talk) with a girl. On __________ (see) me, he introduced the girl to me. I was too embarrassed __________ (say) a word. I didn't expect ______________ (meet) a date in my dirty clothes and mismatched shoes. However, the nice girl did not mind ________________ (have) lunch with me. Although I was a bit ashamed of my style, I had a great time __________________ (eat) with her. I learned that I need _________________ (prepare) better for any surprises hidden in the course of life.

Grammar Tips!

영어에서는 동사의 목적어로 to infinitive (to부정사)와 gerund (동명사)를 취할 수 있다. 하지만 동사에 따라 어떤 동사는 to부정사만을 또 다른 동사는 동명사를 목적어로 취하며, 둘 다 사용할 수 있는 동사들이 있다. 이러한 차이는 특별한 규칙이 없기 때문에 영어를 많이 읽고 접하면서 자연스럽게 익혀가야만 한다.

A. Gerund

(a) He is **exercising** at the gym now.
(b) Look at the **smiling** baby.

(c) **Exercising** is good for your health.
(d) He enjoys **exercising** early in the morning.
(e) Mary is tired of **exercising** after two hours.

In English, there are two types of 'verb+ ~ing'. One is present participle (현재분사) and the other is gerund (동명사). Present participle is used to indicate present progressive (현재진행형), as in (a) or to modify a noun as in (b). On the other hand, a gerund functions as a noun in a sentence. That is, a gerund can be a subject. Also, a gerund can be used as an object of a verb or preposition. In sentence (c), 'exercising' is the subject. In (d), 'exercising' is used as an object of the main verb, 'enjoy'. In (e), 'exercising' functions as an object of the preposition 'of'.

1. Common English Verbs followed by gerunds

(a) Sung-joon avoided telling the truth. (O)
(b) Sung-joon avoided to tell the truth. (X)

As you see above, the verb 'avoid' is followed by a gerund (telling), not an infinitive (to tell). Unfortunately, there is no specific rule to determine which verbs are followed by gerunds or infinitives. Therefore, you need to remember them by using them.

(a) Tom finally gave up asking her out.
(b) Don't avoid telling me the truth.
(c) He enjoys working by himself.
(d) Have you finished eating dinner?
(e) Would you like to discuss implementing the project?

Verbs that require gerund as an object

enjoy appreciate mind forbid	quit/give up finish/get through stop tolerate	avoid postpone/put off delay keep/keep on	consider discuss mention suggest

Grammar Tips!

Stop 이라는 동사는 뒤에 to 부정사와 동명사를 모두 목적어로 취할 수 있다. 하지만 이 경우 그 의미가 달라진다. Stop 동사 다음에 동명사가 오면 '-하기를 멈추다, 그만두다' 라는 뜻이지만 뒤에 to 부정사가 따라올 경우 '-하기 위해서 멈추다', 즉 목적을 나타내는 뜻으로 쓰인다. 예를 들면 He stopped eating cookies. (그는 과자를 더 이상 먹지 않았다.) He stopped to eat cookies. (그는 과자를 먹기 위해 멈췄다.)

Practice 1) Complete the following sentences using the given verb.

1. Ricardo is standing at the corner ______________ for the bus. (wait)

2. I spent five hours ______________ my homework last night. (do)

3. The policeman told the drunken driver to stop, but she kept __________. (drive)

4. Would you mind ______________ the window? (close)

5. Jenny isn't used to _________________ a long dress. (wear)

2. Preposition combinations followed by gerunds

(a) He's interested **in** studying physics.
(b) I look forward **to** hearing from you soon.
(c) She dreamed **of/about** becoming a movie director.
(d) Don't blame him **for** using the money to help the orphans in the deserted area.
(e) Has she insisted **on** changing the plan?

A gerund is also used as an object of a preposition that precedes the gerund. While it is not very hard to use a gerund after a preposition, selecting a proper preposition is quite a challenge! The following is a list of useful preposition combinations.

Verb + preposition combinations followed by gerunds

be excited about be worried about	apologize for blame (sb) for forgive (sb) for have an excuse for have a reason for be responsible for thank (sb) for	believe in be interested in participate in succeed in	be accustomed to in addition to be committed to be devoted to look forward to object to be opposed to be used to
care about complain about/of dream about/of talk about/of think about/of	keep (sb) from prevent (sb) from prohibit (sb) from stop (sb) from	be accused of be capable of for the purpose of be guilty of instead of take advantage of take care of be tired of	insist on plan on depend on concentrate on

3. Idiomatic expressions using gerunds

I **go shopping** every Friday.	'Go~ing' expresses recreational activities.
Please turn off the light **by pushing** the button.	'By ~ing' expresses how something is done.
She **had a great time talking** with them. They **had fun watching** the movie.	'Have a good time/have fun' is followed by a gerund.
Jinsu **had trouble solving** the problem.	'Have trouble/have a difficult time' is followed by a gerund.
Tom **stood in front of his girlfriend's house holding** a pink rose. Hyung-ju **lay in bed reading** the magazine last night.	'stand/sit/lie + place + ~ing' explains specific actions.

I had to **spend most of my vacation working** at the camp.	'spend/waste + time + ~ing' indicates how certain time has been used (or wasted).
When Tim entered the office, he **found the secretary crying** behind the desk. My boss **caught me shopping** on the Internet at work.	'find/catch + someone +~ing' describes specific action of someone. When the verb 'catch' is used, it also expresses negative feeling.

Practice 2) Complete the sentences by filling in the blanks with proper words. Write a proper preposition in the first blank and fill in the second blank using the given verb.

1. The snow prevented them __________ ____________ (visit) their uncle.

2. My father insisted __________ ____________ (go) to the Chinese restaurant.

3. The woman was accused __________ ____________ (kill) her neighbor.

4. Younghee is not responsible __________ ____________ (lead) the group.

B. To Infinitive

(a) My brother promised to come back before 9 pm.
(b) I hope to see you again soon.
(c) Minhee pretended to be sick.

(d) Mr. Kim ran very fast to catch a bus.
(e) Yoon studies hard not to fail the exam again.

(f) There are many things to learn from her.
(g) She has enough time to babysit her sister's son.

'To + verb' is called 'to infinitive' and it has three functions in a sentence: noun, adverb, or adjective. In sentences (a), (b), and (c), 'to infinitive' is used as a noun, that is, an object of the main verb. In sentences (d) and (e), 'to infinitive' is used as an adverb to express purpose (~위하여) modifying the main verb. In sentences (f) and (g), 'to infinitive' modifies the noun that precedes 'to infinitive', functioning as an adjective.

1. Common English Verbs followed by 'to infinitive'

(a) I want to hear his voice. (O)
(b) I want hearing his voice. (X)
(c) I want to hearing his voice. (X)

There are some verbs that require 'to infinitive' as an object. If you use a gerund with these verbs, the sentence is not correct. For example, sentence (b) is not correct because the verb 'want' requires 'to infinitive' as an object, not a gerund. Sentence (c) is also a frequently made mistake.

Verbs followed by 'to infinitive'

Verb + To infinitive			
hope to plan to intend to decide to	promise to agree to offer to refuse to	seem to appear to pretend to ask to	expect to would like to want to need to

2. Verbs followed by 'object + to infinitive'

(a) I would like to visit France. (난 프랑스에 가보면 좋겠다.)
(b) I would like you to visit France. (난 네가 프랑스에 가보면 좋겠다.)

In case of (a), if the sentence comes true, it will be 'I' who will visit France, whereas in (b) it will be 'you' who will visit France.

Grammar Tips!

영어에서 동사 바로 다음에 to 부정사가 오는 경우가 있고 동사 뒤에 사람 목적어가 나오고 다음에 to 부정사가 따라오는 경우가 있다. 문장의 형식으로 볼 때 동사 바로 뒤에 to 부정사가 오는 것은 3형식 (SVO)이고, 동사 뒤에 사람 목적어가 온 뒤 다음에 to 부정사가 오는 것은 5형식 (SVOC)이다. 5형식에 쓰이는 to 부정사의 경우, 목적어로 쓰인 사람 혹은 사물이 to 부정사의 의미상의 주어의 역할을 한다. 예를 들어 I want to eat ice cream. 이라고 하면 원하는 것과 먹는 것의 주체가 모두 I 로서 '내가 아이스크림을 먹고 싶다'는 의미가 되지만, I want you to eat the ice cream. 이라고 하면 본 동사의 주체는 I 이지만 아이스크림을 먹을 주체는 you 가 되어, '난 네가 아이스크림 먹었으면 좋겠어.' 라는 뜻이 된다.

● More examples to compare different uses of 'to infinitive'

(a) I plan to study abroad next year.
(b) The baby wanted to have more milk.

(c) The principal warned the students to behave themselves.
(d) Getting in the program requires me to study day and night.

Verbs that are followed by an object + 'to infinitive'

Verb + (sb) + To infinitive			
tell (sb) to advise (sb) to* encourage (sb) to invite (sb) to	permit (sb) to allow (sb) to warn (sb) to order (sb) to	force (sb) to ask (sb) to need (sb) to	would like (sb) to remind (sb) to require (sb) to

*advise 동사 다음에 바로 동사가 올 때는 ~ing (동명사) 가 오지만, 사람이 목적어인 경우는 advise + sb + to V 의 형태로 쓰인다. 한 가지 예를 보면 He advised selling the old car.
He advised me to sell the old car.

3. Verbs followed by 'gerund' and 'to infinitive'

(a) It began to snow.
 = It began snowing
(b) I hated to study English.
 = I hated studying English.

(c) I remembered to send the letter.
 (난 편지를 보내야 하는 것을 기억했다.)
(d) I remembered sending the letter.
 (난 편지 보냈던 것을 기억했다.)
(e) I regret to tell you the bad news.
 (나쁜 소식을 전하게 되어 유감입니다.)
(f) I regret telling her the secret.
 (그녀에게 비밀을 말한 것을 후회한다.)

(g) I tried to contact her several times.
(그녀와 접촉하려고 여러 번 애썼다.)
(h) I tried contacting her after a while.
(얼마 후에 난 그녀와의 연락을 시도했다.)

In English, some verbs are followed by either a gerund or 'to infinitive' without changing meaning as in (a) and (b). Others change the meaning of the sentence as in (c) through (h). When a verb is followed by 'to infinitive', the object indicates something that should happen afterward (~ 할 것). However, if the verb is followed by a gerund, the object indicates something that happened in the past (~ 했던 것). Also, when the verb 'try' is followed by 'to infinitive', it means 'to make efforts to do something' (~하려고 노력하다. 애쓰다), while if the verb is followed by a gerund, it has the meaning of trying (시험 삼아 ~해보다).

Practice 3) Complete the sentences with the correct form(s) of the verbs in the parenthesis.

1. I always remember ______________________ (turn off) the light before I leave.

2. She promised ____________________ (study) harder for the next exam.

3. Have you ever regretted __________________ (make) a bad decision?

4. He did not avoid _________________ (speak up) in front of the audience.

5. The teacher advised him __________________ (prepare) for the competition.

Practice 4) Unscramble the following words to make a grammatically correct sentence. To do so, you need to change a verb form to either a 'gerund' or 'to infinitive' according to the main verb of each sentence.

1. ____________________
(avoided, the, Kim, change, schedule)

2. ____________________
(again, my, bring, I, class, to, forgot, textbook)

3. ____________________
(friends, join, club, asked, me, reading, my, the)

4. ____________________
(this, advises, stock, boss, week, sell, the, more)

5. ____________________
(sick, I, your, say, father, very, regret, that, is)

3. Useful expressions using 'to infinitive'

(a) He came to Korea to meet his friends.
= He came to Korea in order to meet his friends.
= He came to Korea so as to meet his friends.
(b) He came to Korea for meeting his friends. (X)

(c) I am very happy to see you again.
(d) He was anxious to tell the truth in front of the detective.
(e) Mary was sad to hear that he left the town.

(f) She was too young to watch the movie.
= She was so young that she could not watch the movie.
(g) It was too heavy for Jim to lift the box.
= It was so heavy that Jim could not lift the box.
=The box was so heavy that Jim could not lift it.

(h) Mr. Bob is rich enough to buy an old castle.
= Mr. Bob has enough money to buy an old castle.

Grammar Tips!

To 부정사는 종종 동사의 목적을 표현하기 위해 사용되며 (-하기 위하여) 이렇게 사용된 to 부정사는 in order to + V 혹은 so as to + V 와 바꾸어 쓸 수 있다. 목적을 나타내는 표현을 만들 때 만들기 쉬운 실수는 for + -ing 을 사용하는 것이다. 예를 들어 I worked hard for making money. 란 표현은 어색하며, 대신에 I worked hard to make money. 라고 해야 한다. 또한 영어에서는 특정 감정이나 느낌을 나타내는 형용사 (happy, glad, pleased, excited) 다음에 to 부정사를 사용하기도 한다. (예: I am so happy to meet you here.) 그리고 영어 문장 중에 'too +형용사 + to 부정사' 의 구문이 있는데 이것은 '너무-해서 ~할 수 없다' 라는 부정문을 만든다. 예를 들어 She is too young to watch the movie. (그녀는 너무 어려서 그 영화를 볼 수 없다)를 보면 문장 내에 부정어 (not) 가 들어가 있지 않지만 의미상 부정이 된 다는 것에 주의해야 한다. 이것을 다르게 바꾸면 She is so young that she can't watch the movie. 라고 할 수 있다. 마지막으로 영어에서 enough 라는 표현을 쓸 때 '-하기에 충분한' 이란 의미를 가지며 어순을 보면 형용사 뒤에 그리고 명사 앞에 enough 를 넣는다. 그리고 뒤에 to 부정사가 따라 온다. 예를 보면, She is busy enough to hire an assistant. (그녀는 비서를 고용할 만큼 충분히 바쁘다.) 혹은 He had enough time to follow her business trip. (그는 그녀의 출장에 따라갈 만큼 시간이 충분했다.)

4. Different forms of 'to infinitive' and a gerund

(a) I am happy to meet you. (b) I am happy to have met you yesterday.	(c) I appreciate talking to the CEO. (d) I appreciate having talked with the CEO.
(e) He wants to invite Mary to the party. (f) He wants to be invited to the party.	(g) Thank you for inviting me to the party. (h) I forgot being invited to the party.

When the action in 'to infinitive' or the gerund happens at a different time from the main verb, to have + pp as in (b) or having + pp as in (d) is used respectively. Also, if the subject is a passive agent of 'to infinitive' or a gerund, to be + pp as in (f) or being + pp as in (h) is used respectively. The following shows the patterns to express different cases.

	Referring to the same time	Referring to a different time
Active	to see seeing	to have seen having seen
Passive	to be seen being seen	to have been seen having been seen

Practice 5) Correct the mistake in each sentence.

1. She was too sick walking to the store.

➲

2. The children were enough young to get free admissions.

➲

3. I want being invited to Jane's party.

➲

4. Mark woke up early for catching the first train.

➲

5. I don't enjoy laughing at by other people.

➲

5. Other usage of gerund and infinitive

(a) I saw a baby cry on the street.
(b) I saw a baby crying on the street.
(c) I heard him sing everyday.
(d) I heard him singing on the rainy day.

(e) My mother did not let me drive the car.
(f) She made the child take the medicine.
(g) She had the child take the medicine.
(h) His friend helped him move the boxes.
  = His friend helped him to move the boxes
(i) She got the child to take the medicine.

(j) I had him repair the watch.
(k) I had the watch repaired.
  = I got the watch repaired.

When you use verbs of perception (지각동사– see, watch, hear, feel), a base verb form is used as an object complement as in (a) and (c). These base verb forms are called bare infinitive (원형 부정사). However, if you want to express something that is in progress with the verbs of perception, use '~ing' (present participle) to express something is happening at the moment. Also, there are verbs that take base verb forms as an object complement: **let, make**, and **have**. (사역동사) as in (e) to (g). These verbs mean 'to cause somebody to do something'. Similarly, the verb 'help' can be followed by either a bare infinitive or 'to infinitive' as in (h). In case of the verb 'get', 'to infinitive' is always followed, and it has the meaning of **persuasion** as in (i). When the object of the sentence is a thing, not a person, past participle (pp) can be used instead of a base verb form as in (k) to express passive meaning.

Practice 6) Correct the errors in the sentences. Each sentence has one error.

1. My mother made me to take the medicine.
   ☞ Correction:

2. When I went to shopping last Monday, I saw a man walking with Jane.
   ☞ Correction:

3. I asked my friend to let me to use his dictionary.
   ☞ Correction:

4. I am looking forward to hear from you soon.
   ☞ Correction:

5. She left early in the morning to meeting her boyfriend.
   ☞ Correction:

Unit in a Nutshell

- As an object of a verb, use 'to infinitive' or gerunds. However, different verbs take different forms of objects.
- A gerund often follows a 'verb + preposition' combination as an object of the preposition. Try to remember as many 'verb + preposition' combinations as you can.
- Using 'to infinitive' or gerunds, you can express various ideas. Remember their usage and specific forms introduced in this unit.

Writing in Action

My Vacation Wishes: Writing a letter

You are going to write a letter to your best friend to talk about your next vacation plans and wishes. In your letter, include specific plans and explain why you want to do them. Use gerunds and 'to infinitive' to explain your ideas and reasons.

To generate ideas for the writing, first ask yourself the following questions.

(1) What do you really want to do? List up to three things.

(2) Choose 1 or 2 wishes you want to do most. What do you need to do or prepare to make the wishes come true?

(3) Why do you want to do them? Give a detailed explanation.

(4) How would you feel after you accomplish the plans?

____

Dear ______________________,

____

____

____

____

____

____

____

____

____

____

____

____

____

____

Unit 8 Answer Key

Test yourself! (p. 137)

When I got in the café, I found my friend talking with a girl. On seeing me, he introduced the girl to me. I was too embarrassed to say a word. I didn't expect to meet a date in my dirty clothes and mismatched shoes. However, the nice girl did not mind having lunch with me. Although I was a bit ashamed of my style, I had a great time eating with her. I learned that I need to prepare better for any surprises hidden in the course of life.

Practice 1) (p. 139)

1. Ricardo is standing at the corner waiting for the bus.
2. I spent five hours doing my homework last night.
3. The policeman told the drunken driver to stop, but she kept driving.
4. Would you mind closing the window?
5. Jenny isn't used to wearing a long dress.

Practice 2) (p. 142)

1. The snow prevented them from visiting their uncle.
2. My father insisted on going to the Chinese restaurant.
3. The woman was accused of killing her neighbor.
4. Younghee is not responsible for leading the group.

Practice 3) (p. 146)

1. I always remember to turn off the light before I leave.

2. She promised to study harder for the next exam.

3. Have you ever regretted making a bad decision?

4. He did not avoid speaking up in front of the audience.

5. The teacher advised him to prepare for the competition.

Practice 4) (p. 147)

1. Kim avoided changing the schedule.
2. I forgot to bring my textbook to class again.
3. My friends asked me to join the reading club.
4. The boss advises selling more stock this week.
5. I regret to say that your father is very sick.

Practice 5) (p. 149)

1. She was too sick to walk to the store.
2. The children were young enough to get free admissions.
3. I want to be invited to Jane's party.
4. Mark woke up early to catch the first train.
5. I don't enjoy being laughed at by other people.

Practice 6) (p. 151)

1. My mother made me take the medicine.
2. When I went shopping last Monday, I saw a man walking with Jane.
3. I asked my friend to let me use his dictionary.
4. I am looking forward to hearing from you soon.
5. She left early in the morning to meet her boyfriend.

Unit 9 Passive Voice

Test yourself!

\# Unscramble the given words in the correct order. Use proper punctuation in the end.

(1) ______________________________

(flat, been, has, cleaned, by, the, flatmate, my)

(2) ______________________________

(computer, the, being, used, is, at, moment, the)

(3) ______________________________

(are, accidents, by, many, caused, dangerous, driving)

(4) ______________________________

(something, done, be, must, before, late, it's, too)

(5) ______________________________

(found, that, we, the, had, game, cancelled, been)

Grammar Tips!

영어에서 수동태문장은 누가 했는가보다 무엇이 행해졌는가가 더 중요할 때 사용되며, 기본적으로 be + pp 형태를 쓴다. 수동태형을 정확하게 쓰기 위해서는 be동사의 인칭과 시제에 따른 변화형(am, is, are, was, were)과 불규칙 과거분사 pp를 알아야 한다. 그러므로, 영어로 된 글을 많이 읽고, 연습을 통해 숙지하도록 한다.

A. Passive Voice 1 (S + V + O)

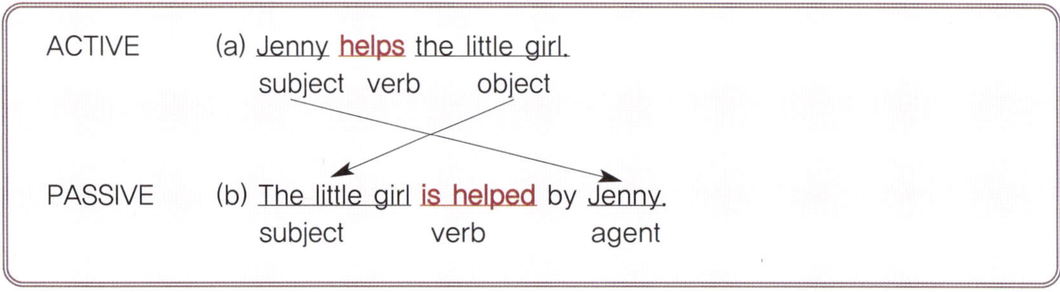

We generally use an active verb to express what the subject does as in (a). However, when 'what happens' is more important than 'who does it,' we use the passive voice.

To make the passive voice, the object of the active verb becomes the subject of the passive verb. The little girl in (a) becomes the subject of the passive verb in (b).

The active verb 'helps' is changed to 'is helped'. Also, the subject in the active voice comes after 'by' in the passive sentence. The noun which follows 'by' is called the agent. In (b), Jenny is the agent.

ACTIVE	(a) A terrible accident *happened*.
PASSIVE	(b) (none)

Remember that only transitive verbs (타동사) are used in the passive voice. Transitive verbs are verbs which take an object: help, make, eat, want, etc. However, it is not possible to use intransitive verbs (자동사) in the passive voice. Intransitive verbs are verbs which do not take an object: happen, sleep, come, seem, appear, etc.

Grammar Tips!

수동태문장은 동사가 타동사(목적어를 항상 취하는 동사)일 때 만들어지며 행위자에 의해 어떤 일이 되어질 수 있다. 그러나 자동사(목적어를 취하지 않고 주어가 직접 능동적 행위를 하거나, 주어를 보충 설명하는 보어를 사용하는 동사)는 수동태문장에서 쓰일 수 없다.

ACTIVE	(a) Most of the students laughed at the boy.
PASSIVE	(b) The boy was laughed at by most of the students.
	(c) The boy was laughed by most of the students. (x)
ACTIVE	(d) The nurses took care of the wounded.
PASSIVE	(e) The wounded were taken care of by the nurses.
ACTIVE	(f) The company has put off the payment.
PASSIVE	(g) The payment has been put off by the company.

As you see in the examples above, some verbal phrases, such as bring up, turn off, and look at, must stay together to form a passive verb. Do not drop the adverb or preposition at the end of the phrase as in (c).

Practice 1) Complete the sentences with proper words and expressions.

1. This morning our teacher ________________ (arrive) ten minutes late.

2. Our newspaper ________________ (read) by over 300,000 people every day.

3. This isn't my jacket. It ________________ (belong) to Sara.

4. A new apartment complex ________________ (build) next to our building next year.

5. The children ______________________ (take care of) by their grandparents last summer.

1. How to make affirmative statements using the passive voice

(a) Tony **opens** the window.
→ The window **is opened** by Tony.
(b) Tony **opened** the window.
→ The window **was opened** by Tony.
(c) Tony **will open** the window.
→ The window **will be opened** by Tony.

(d) Tony **has opened** the window.
→ The window **has been opened** by Tony.
(e) Tony **had opened** the window.
→ The window **had been opened** by Tony.

(f) Tony **is opening** the window.
→ The window **is being opened** by Tony.
(g) Tony **was opening** the window.
→ The window **was being opened** by Tony.

When you change the active voice sentences (a) and (b) into the passive voice, pay attention to the tense and subject/number agreement. If there is a modal verb like 'will', 'can', 'should', 'must', the passive form is modal + be + pp as in (c). For the present/past perfect tense, change have/has/had + pp to have/has/had + been + pp as in (d) and (e). When the progressive tense is used, the passive form is be + being + pp as in sentences (f) and (g).

2. How to make negative statements using the passive voice

(a) Tony does not open the window.
→ The window is not opened by Tony.
(b) Tony did not open the window.
→ The window was not opened by Tony.
(c) Tony will not open the window.
→ The window will not be opened by Tony.

(d) Tony has not opened the window.
→ The window has not been opened by Tony.
(e) Tony had not opened the window.
→ The window had not been opened by Tony.

(f) Tony is not opening the window.
→ The window is not being opened by Tony.
(g) Tony was not opening the window.
→ The window was not being opened by Tony.

In the negative passive sentences, pay attention to the position of 'NOT.' It has to be the second word of the verb phrase as you see the examples above.

3. How to make questions using the passive voice

(a) Does she make the box?
→ She makes the box. (Affirmative statement: Active voice)
→ The box is made by her. (Passive voice)
→ Is the box made by her? (Passive voice in question)

(b) Did Tony open the windows?
→ Tony opened the windows. (Affirmative statement: Active voice)
→ The windows were opened by Tony. (Passive voice)
→ Were the windows opened by Tony? (Passive voice in question)

(c) Has Tony finished the project?
→ Tony has finished the project. (Affirmative statement: Active voice)
→ The project has been finished by Tony. (Passive voice)
→ Has the project been finished by Tony? (Passive voice in question)

(d) When did he invent the telephone?
→ He invented the telephone when. (x)
→ The telephone was invented by him when. (x) (Passive voice)
→ Was the telephone invented by him when? (x) (Passive voice)
→ When was the telephone invented (by him)? (Passive voice in question)

(e) Who invented the telephone?
→ Who invented the telephone. (x)
→ The telephone was invented by whom. (x) (Passive voice)
→ Was the telephone invented by whom? (x) (Passive voice)
→ By whom was the telephone invented? (Passive voice in question)
→ Who was the telehone invented by?

When you change the questions into the passive voice, there are three different ways to make them. As you see in (a) and (b), the passive voice questions start with Be + S + pp?. The questions with perfect tense start with Have/Has/Had + S + been + pp? in the passive voice. If there is a 'wh-word' in the question, the sentence starts with the 'wh-word' : Wh-word + be + S + pp?

Grammar Tips!

수동태 문장 **be + pp**에서는 be동사가 시제를 나타내고, 완료수동태 have/has/had+been+pp에서는 시제와 인칭에 주의하여 have/has/had중 하나를 선택하면 된다. 의문문에서는 **be + pp**가 기본형이기 때문에 be동사가 문장에서 가장 먼저 쓰이지만, 완료수동태에서는 조동사인 have/has/had가, 의문사가 있는 경우에는 의문사가 문두에 온다.

Practice 2) Change the sentences into the passive voice.

1. He loves her.

2. She doesn't love him.

3. We loved them.

4. Do they love us?

5. You should help the poor boy.

6. Who did you invite to your party?

B. Passive Voice 2 (S + V + IO + DO)

(a) The witness gave the police (IO) some information (DO).

→ The police were given some information by the witness.

→ Some information was given to the police by the witness.

(b) My parents bought my brother (IO) an expensive bike (DO).

→ My brother was bought an expensive bike by my parents. (X)

→ An expensive bike was bought for my brother by my parents. (O)

*IO = indirect object   DO = direct object

Either an indirect object or a direct object may become the subject of a passive voice sentence. Notice that some verbs (buy, write, get, cook, make, choose, find, bring) only take a direct object as a subject in the passive voice.

Practice 3) Change the sentences to the passive voice.

1. The company offered Mike a wonderful job.

→

→

2. I didn't ask him such stupid questions.

→

→

3. The professor told the students surprising news.

→

→

C. Passive Voice 3 (S + V + O + OC)

(a) His announcement made all of us happy.
O OC
→ All of us were made happy by his announcement.

(b) The citizens elected him president.
O OC
→ He was elected president by the citizens.

(c) Sam and I saw some boys swim in the river.
O OC
→ Some boys were seen to swim in the river by Sam and me.

(d) They made him go there alone.
O OC
→ He was made to go there alone (by them).

(e) The children helped the kitten to get out of the box.
O OC
→ The kitten was helped to get out of the box by the children.

When you change the sentences with this pattern, be sure to make an active object into a passive subject with the complement following. Notice that some verbs like see, watch, hear, make, have, let, always take a bare infinitive (원형부정사) in active sentences. However, these verbs always take 'to infinitive' as a complement when they are used in passive sentences. For example, in sentence (c), the verb saw in the active voice becomes were seen and the objective complement swim becomes to swim.

Grammar Tips!

S+V+O+OC의 문형인 경우, 지각동사(see, watch, hear등)과 사역동사(make, have, let)가 수동태 문장으로 바뀌는 경우는 목적보어인 원형부정사는 항상 to부정사로 바뀌게 된다. 만약 목적보어가 현재분사(V~ing)인 경우는 그대로 현재분사를 사용한다.

Practice 4) Change the sentences into passive.

1. We named our puppy Happy.

2. Her friends call her Ice Princess.

3. The jury found the suspect guilty of fraud.

4. He heard her singing some of the old pop songs.

5. The coach made him run faster for a good record.

Practice 5) Correct the error in each sentence. Each sentence has one error.

1. The singer were made popular by the talk show.

   ☞ Correction:

2. An airplane was saw flying under the cloud.

   ☞ Correction:

3. He was expect to arrive in time.

   ☞ Correction:

4. She not is allowed to go out late at night.

   ☞ Correction:

D. Passive Voice 4 (It is said that ~)

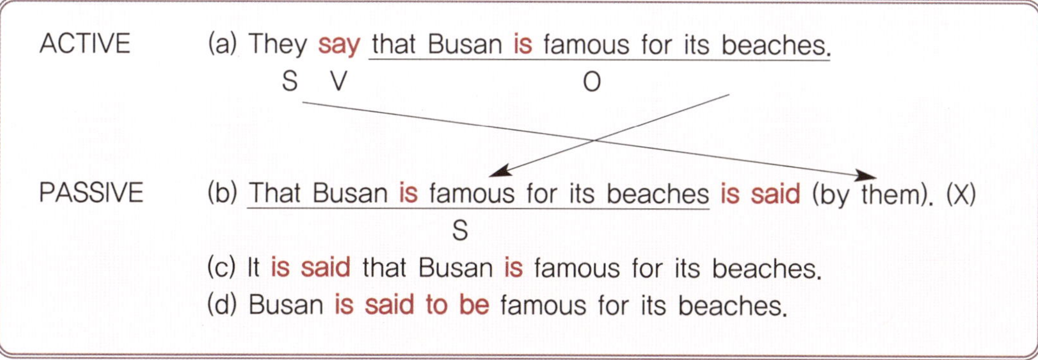

ACTIVE	(e) People **believe** that Mr. Johnson **owned** the largest house in the town.
PASSIVE	(f) That Mr. Johnson **owned** the largest house in the town **is believed** (by people). (X)
	(g) It **is believed** that Mr. Johnson **owned** the largest house in the town.
	(h) Mr. Johnson **is believed to have owned** the largest house in the town.

Some complex sentences like the sentence (a) can be changed into two different passive voices as in (c) and (d). Through sentence (b), sentence (a) becomes (c) with the subject 'it' (가주어). When you compare the verb tenses, the verb in the main clause 'is said' and the verb in the subordinate clause 'is' are both present tense. Next you can replace 'it' (가주어) with 'Busan', which is the subject of the subordinate clause in sentence (c). Then use the 'to infinitive' 'to be'.

You can use these structures with a number of other verbs: allege, consider, expect, know, report, think, understand.

Grammar Tips!

영어에서는 문장의 주어가 너무 긴 것을 피하는 경향이 있는데, 위의 일부 동사(allege 이하)가 문장의 본동사로 쓰여 명사절을 목적어로 취하는 경우 수동태문장에서 명사절을 주어로 쓰는 대신 가주어 it를 사용하고 문장 끝부분에 명사절 진주어를 놓는다. 또 명사절의 주어를 수동태 문장의 주어로 문장을 만들 수 있는데, 주어 + be + pp + **to V** (명사절 속의 동사)의 형태로 쓴다. 이때 be동사의 시제는 능동태 문장의 본동사시제와 일치시킨다. 만약 주절의 시제(현재)와 종속절의 시제(과거)가 다른 경우, 주어 + be + pp + **to have pp**의 형태를 사용한다. 예를 들어 (e)의 주절의 동사 believe와 종속절의 owned가 '현재-과거'로 다르기 때문에 to 부정사를 쓰는 (h) 문장으로 바뀔때는 'to have owned'가 된다.

Practice 6) Change the following sentences into two different passive sentences.

1. People expect that the book will be published soon.

→

→

2. The police reported the three men killed a bear in the mountain.

→

→

3. We know that the rich man met the poor girl.

→

→

Unit in a Nutshell

- Passive voice is used when the subject (who) is less important than what happens.
- Passive voice is made in the form of 'be + pp (past participle)', and 'be verb' should agree with the tense and number of the subject.

Practice 7) Underline the verb phrase with active voice and circle the verb phrases with passive voice.

1. Our class is being taught by Dr. Smith.

2. Look, this is a secret. Come inside where we won't be overheard.

3. A: Have you paid your phone bill yet?

B: No, I haven't. If I don't, my phone will be disconnected by the phone company.

4. When I got home, I could see that the vegetables in my garden had been watered every day, and the grass had been cut regularly.

Practice 8) Correct or Incorrect?

Read the following sentences. If it is correct, circle C. If it is not correct, circle IC. If you circle IC, correct the mistake.

1. One thousand people are employed by the company. (C IC)

☞ Correction:

2. When I was on vacation, my digital camera was disappeared from my hotel room. (C IC)

☞ Correction:

3. When I was on vacation, my digital camera was stolen from my hotel room. (C IC)

☞ Correction:

4. There were some problems at first, but they seem to have solved. (C IC)

☞ Correction:

5. I offered the job, but I refused it. (C IC)

☞ Correction:

6. The prices of all our products have been reduced in the sale this year.

(C IC)

☞ Correction:

7. They are said that they work 14 hours a day. (C IC)

☞ Correction:

Writing in Action

Task 1.

Complete the following story by filling in the blanks with proper words.

Zoos in Korea

Almost everyone __________ (enjoy) visiting a zoo. Today zoos are common. The first zoo in Korea ____________ (establish) in 1909 in Changkyungwon, which was transformed from Changkyung Palace. It was the fourth zoo in Asia to open to the public. It ___________ (love) by the public for 75 years when it moved to Seoul Grand Zoo in Kwacheon in 1984.

Seoul Grand Zoo is the only global scale zoo in Korea and _____________ (hold) more than 3,272 animals in 377 species. Everland in Kyounggi-do, which ____________ (call) Youngin Jayeon Nongwon in 1976, ________________ (have) 4,500 animals in more than 200 species and __________ (succeed) in being the first zoo to hold lions and tigers in the same safari.

Zoos in Korea usually ____________ (open) in parks or amusement parks and _____________________ (show) animals on display in a locked cage. They ________________ (become) a good place for field trips for young children.

Task 2.

Write one or two paragraphs to report an accident that you saw or you were involved in. Include at least three passive voice sentences in your writing.

To generate ideas for the writing, first ask yourself the following questions.

1) What happened in the accident?
2) Who was involved in it?
3) When and where did it happen?

Unit 9 Answer Key

Test yourself! (p. 157)

(1) The flat has been cleaned by my flatmate.

(2) The computer is being used at the moment.

(3) Many accidents are caused by dangerous driving.

(4) Something must be done before it's too late.

(5) We found that the game had been cancelled.

Practice 1) (p. 160)

1. This morning our teacher **arrived** ten minutes late.
2. Our newspaper **is read** by over 300,000 people every day.
3. This isn't my jacket. It **belongs** to Sara.
4. A new apartment complex **will be built** next to our building next year.
5. The children **were taken care of** by their grandparents last summer.

Practice 2) (p. 163)

1. She is loved by him.
2. He is not loved by her.
3. They were loved by us.
4. Are we loved by them?
5. The poor boy should be helped by you.
6. Who was invited to your party (by you)?

Practice 3) (p. 164)

1. Mike was offered a wonderful job by the company.

   A wonderful job was offered to Mike by the company.

2. He was not asked such stupid questions by me.

   Such stupid questions were not asked of him by me.

3. The students were told surprising news by the professor.

   Surprising news was told to the students by the professor.

Practice 4) (p. 166)

1. Our puppy was named Happy (by us).
2. She is called Ice Princess by her friends.
3. The suspect was found guilty of fraud by the jury.
4. She was heard singing some of the old pop songs (by him).
5. He was made to run faster for a good record by the coach.

Practice 5) (p. 167)

1. The singer **was made** popular by the talk show.
2. An airplane **was seen** flying under the cloud.
3. He **was expected** to arrive in time.
4. She **isn't** allowed to go out late at night.

Practice 6) (p. 169)

1. It is expected that the book will be published soon.

   The book is expected to be published soon.

2. It was reported that the three men killed a bear in the mountain.

   The three men were reported to kill a bear in the mountain.

3. It is known that the rich man met the poor girl.
The rich man is known to have met the poor girl.

Practice 7) (p. 169)

1. Our class is being taught by Dr. Smith.
2. Look, this is a secret. Come inside where we won't be overheard.
3. A: Have you paid your phone bill yet?
   B: No, I haven't. If I don't, my phone will be disconnected by the phone company.
4. When I got home, I could see that the vegetables in my garden had been watered every day, and the grass had been cut regularly.

Practice 8) (p. 170)

1. C
2. IC : was disappeared → disappeared
3. C
4. IC : have solved → have been solved
5. IC : offered → was offered
6. C
7. IC : They are said → It is said that they work 14 hours a day.
   → They are said to work 14 hours a day.

Task 1. (p. 171)

Zoos in Korea

Almost everyone **enjoys** visiting a zoo. Today zoos are common. The first zoo in Korea **was established** in 1909 in Changkyungwon, which was transformed from Changkyung Palace. It was the fourth zoo in Asia to open to the public. It **had been loved** by the public for 75 years when it moved to Seoul Grand Zoo in Kwacheon in 1984.

Seoul Grand Zoo is the only global scale zoo in Korea and **holds** more than 3,272 animals in 377 species. Everland in Kyounggi-do, which **was called** (call) Youngin Jayeon Nongwon in 1976, **has** 4,500 animals in more than 200 species and **succeeded** in being the first zoo to hold lions and tigers in the same safari.

Zoos in Korea usually **open** in parks or amusement parks and **show** animals on display in a locked cage. They **have become** a good place for field trips for young children.

Unit 10 Punctuation and Capitalization

Test yourself!

Complete each sentence with appropriate punctuations and capital letters.

(1) People worship different animals such as the bird the dog and the cow

(2) william is confident and he will live a successful life

(3) i am not tired therefore i can do more work

(4) We have fun by playing games dancing and singing

(5) st. mary's college is located in boston, massachusetts

(6) My friend and I are taking english 101 class every thursday

(7) americans celebrate thanksgiving in november

Grammar Tips!

흔히 문장 부호(punctuations)와 대/소문자(capitalizations)의 구분은 중요하지 않게 생각되어 생략하거나 기본 규칙에 어긋나게 쓰일 때가 많다. 그러나 올바르지 않은 문장 부호와 대문자의 사용은 문장의 명확도를 떨어뜨리므로, 문법적으로 복잡한 장문을 쓰는 것보다 바른 문장 부호(, ; : . ? !)와 대문자의 사용(요일, 달, 언어, 사람/장소등의 고유명사, 나라, 국적, I, 문장의 첫 단어 등)이 기본 영작의 중요한 요소라 하겠다. 그러므로 쉬운 것이라 대충 지나치지 말고 기본규칙은 반드시 알아둘 것!

A. How to use commas

1. To separate three or more words, phrases, or clauses written in a series

(a) I like apples, bananas, and strawberries. (Noun)

(b) The audience laughed, cheered, and applauded throughout the performance. (Verb)

(c) The council responded to the emergency quickly, responsibly, and maturely. (Adverb)

(d) We did some sightseeing, ate some great food, and took a lot of photos. (Phrase)

2. To separate independent clauses when they are joined by any of these seven coordinating conjunctions: for, and, nor, but, or, yet, so (FANBOYS)

(a) I did not go to the party, for I had a lot of assignments that night.
(b) I went to Alaska with my college mates, and we had such a wonderful time.
(c) I do not like meat, nor do I eat fish. (nor + V + S: 주어 동사 도치에 유의)
(d) My friends seemed to be excited, but I felt frightened.

(e) You have to study hard, or you will not be able to pass the exam.
(f) He doesn't like mathematics, yet he majored in physics.

3. After a conjunctive adverb: therefore, however, thus, nevertheless, consequently, finally

(a) Your grades are excellent. Therefore, we would like to offer you a scholarship.
(b) John studied hard day and night. Nevertheless, he did not receive good grades.

4. Before and after a conjunctive adverb that is placed inside an independent clause

(a) Jen worked many hours. She, however, does not make much money.

5. When a dependent clause is placed at the beginning of a sentence, place a comma between the independent clause and the dependent clause. Some dependent clause markers are: because, since, when, while, until, if, as, though, although, unless, after, before, once, whether.

(a) While I was eating, the cat scratched at the door.
(b) Because her alarm clock was broken, she was late for class.
(c) If you are ill, you ought to see a doctor.
(d) When the snow stops falling, we'll shovel the driveway.

However, do not put a comma after the main clause when a dependent clause follows it, except for cases of extreme contrast using while or whereas.

(a) She was late for class, because her alarm clock was broken. (X)
(b) The cat scratched at the door, while I was eating. (X)
(~하는 동안에)
(c) I like classical music, while (=whereas) my brother likes rock music. (O)
(~하는 반면에)

6. After introductory adverbs or introductory phrases (The phrase may be a prepositional phrase, an infinitive phrase, or a participle phrase.)

(a) Fortunately, every faculty member supported the president.
(b) To pass the driver's test, you must study the handbook.
(c) Having finished the test, he left the room.

7. Appositive (동격어)

(a) Sputnik I, the world's first satellite, was launched by the Soviet Union in 1957.
└ Appositive ┘
(b) Obama, the President of the United Sates, was born in Hawaii.
└ Appositive ┘

8. Between the name of a city and the state or country

(a) The Eiffel Tower in Paris, France is an architectural wonder.
(b) A terrible earthquake hit Kobe, Japan in 1995.

9. Before a relative pronoun clause that is non-essential

(a) Beth, who lives across town, plans to study abroad in Japan.
S (non-essential phrase) V
(b) I am planning to have lobster for dinner, which is one of my favorite kinds of seafood.
S V (non-essential phrase)

A non-essential relative clause provides extra information about the precedent (선행사) it modifies. When the nonessential relative clause comes in the middle of the sentence, make sure you add a comma before and after the clause as in (a). However, do NOT use a comma before the relative clause if it contains essential information about the precedent.

(a) The chocolate cake that I had at John's was delicious.
S (essential phrase) V
(b) People who work in my office are very kind.
S (essential phrase) V
(c) This is a desk, that belongs to me. (x)

An essential clause or phrase is used to modify a noun. It also adds information that is critical to the meaning of the sentence. Remember that a comma should not be used in essential clauses. The relative pronoun 'that' almost always indicates an essential clause; thus, do not use 'that' with a comma.

10. After the salutation of a personal letter or after the closing of a letter

Dear Jane, Sincerely, With love,

Practice 1) Add or delete commas where necessary in the following sentences.

1. Nepal is between India and China.

2. They put garlands around their neck give them special food and make them gifts.

3. James bought an expensive car. Therefore he had to get a car alarm.

4. Before they have the special party they have a church ceremony.

5. My sister likes doing outdoor activities while I like reading books at home.

6. The tsunami hit Telewatta Sri Lanka.

7. Crescent City California is on the coast.

8. I love to wear sneakers which are comfortable.

9. The bus, which I took this morning, broke in the middle of the highway.

10. We are going to move out, because the living conditions are dangerous.

B. How to use semicolons (;)

Semicolons, like all other punctuation marks, ensure clarity in written language by joining independent clauses and separating items in a list. Semicolons are more frequently used in formal written language rather than informal language. Semicolons perform the following basic functions.

1. To join two independent clauses that are closely connected in idea or that have equal emphasis with no connecting words

● Independent clause [;] independent clause [.]

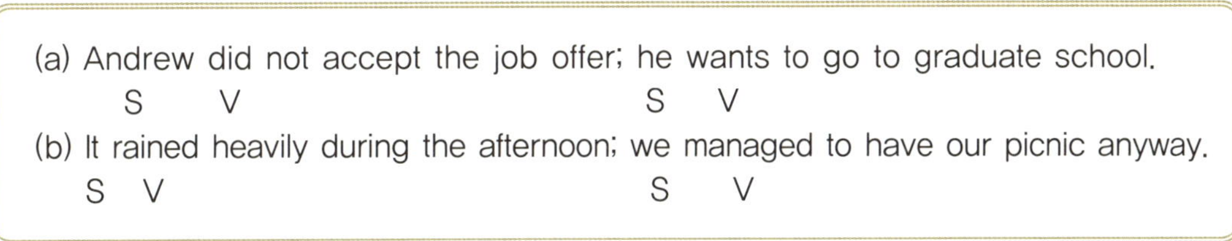

(a) Andrew did not accept the job offer; he wants to go to graduate school.
S V S V

(b) It rained heavily during the afternoon; we managed to have our picnic anyway.
S V S V

2. To join two independent clauses in which the second clause begins with a conjunctive adverb (접속부사)

● Independent clause [;] conjunctive adverb [,] independent clause [.]

(a) The storm yesterday was the worst; however, school did not close.
S V (adverb) S V

(b) Skiing is dangerous; nevertheless, millions of people ski.
S V (adverb) S V

3. To separate items which contain commas in a series

Some of the most well-known cities in the United States include Chicago, Illinois; New York City, New York; Las Vegas, Nevada; and Los Angeles, California.

Practice 2) Add semicolons where necessary and fill in the blanks with proper conjunctive adverbs and correct punctuation.

1. Police kept people away from the scene of the accident; __________, ambulance workers tried to pull victims out of the wreck.

2. Grace works for a prestigious law firm she is their top criminal lawyer.

3. The future of our wild animals is uncertain; _________, illegal shooting and chemical poisoning threaten many birds.

4. Homework is boring therefore, I never do it.

5. John studies hard _________, he is not getting good grades.

6. He thinks 8:00 AM is an unreasonable time for class in contrast, I think it is fine.

C. How to use colon (:)

1. After formal salutations

Dear Ms. Smith:	Dear Soongsil University:

* Use a comma in informal letters → Dear Mom,

2. A list of items

Several survival items should be stored in your storm shelter: food, water, flashlights, batteries, blankets, a radio, and a first-aid kit.

3. Before a long quotation

As Albert C. Baugh and Thomas Cable state in their book *The History of the English Language*: There is no such thing as uniformity in language ...

4. Expressions of time

10:30 AM   2:10 PM

Practice 3) Add colons in appropriate positions to the following texts.

1. Dear Dr. Patterson

2. To check a book out of the library, you should follow this procedure write down the call number of the book, find the book, take it to the circulation desk, fill out the card, and show your student I.D.

3. Martin Luther King, Jr., who was an American activist and well-known leader in the Civil Rights Movement, said in his famous speech I have a dream that my four little children will one day live in a nation where they will not be judged by the color of their skin, but by the content of their character.

D. Apostrophe (')

1. Forming Possessives of Nouns

Add 's to the singular form of the word (even if it ends in -s)

the owner's car
James's hat (James' hat is also acceptable.)

Add 's to the plural forms that do not end in -s

The children's game The geese's honking

Add ' to the end of plural nouns that end in -s

Two cats' toys　　　Three friends' letters

Add 's to the end of compound words

my brother-in-law's money

Add 's to the last noun to show joint possession of an object

Todd and Anne's apartment

2. Showing omission of letters

Apostrophes are used in contractions (단축형). The apostrophe shows the omission of certain letters. Contractions are common in speaking and in informal writing. To use an apostrophe to create a contraction, place an apostrophe where the omitted letter(s) would go. Here are some examples:

don't = do not
I'm = I am
he'll = he will
who's = who is
shouldn't = should not
didn't = did not
could've= could have (NOT 'could of'!)

3. Do not use apostrophes with possessive pronouns.

Apostrophes should not be used with possessive pronouns because possessive pronouns (소유대명사 : my, your, his, her) already show possession.

his' book (X)
his book (O)

a friend of yours' (X)
a friend of yours (O)

The group made it's decision. (X)
The group made its decision. (O)

*Note: Its and it's are not the same.

It's → Contraction of 'It is' It's raining. = It is raining.
Its → A possessive pronoun meaning 'belonging to'
The school made its (= the school's) own policy.

Practice 4) Correct the following sentences.

1. Nathan doesnt like to play basketball.

2. The current economic turmoil is everyone concern.

3. Each office has it's own espresso machine.

4. I like Daniel guitar and his' drum.

5. Its raining outside today.

E. Period (.)

1. Always put a period at the end of a statement.

Today was a great day for me.
I don't know when he came back last night.

* If a sentence is not a statement, the end punctuation can be either a question mark (?) or an exclamation point (!)

How many students do you meet a day?
What a great day!

2. Do NOT use a period after a signature.

Sincerely yours,
Jayoung Kim. (X)
Jayoung Kim (O)

3. Use a period after a conventional abbreviation (=short form).

Mr. the U.S.A. Inc.

F. Rules for Capitalization

1. Always capitalize the first word of a sentence.

Today is not Sunday.
Where did he go?

2. Always capitalize the word 'I'.

John brought the dessert, and I brought some drinks.
I want some tea.
The winners of the contest were Ned and I.

3. Capitalize a title before a proper noun (고유명사).

President Bush Dr. Smith Mr. Park

4. Capitalize the names of people and races.

Bob Caucasian African-American

*Note: Do not capitalize the words black and white that refer to races.
e.g) The blacks and whites in our neighborhood are well integrated.

5. Capitalize the names of religions, deities, and sacred terms.

God Buddhist Catholic Muslim

6. Capitalize geographic locations.

New York Mont Blanc the Ohio River

7. Capitalize nationalities and languages.

Vietnamese Spanish English Japanese

8. Capitalize the titles of books, movies, and essays.

Harry Potter	A Kiss	Days and Nights

*제목(title)을 쓸 경우 주요단어(content words)는 모두 대문자, 기능어(관사, 접속사, 전치사)는 소문자로 쓴다.

9. Capitalize the days of the week, months, and holidays.

Wednesday	August	the Fourth of July

*Do not capitalize the names of the seasons: spring, summer, fall, winter.

10. Capitalize the names of documents, historical events, and organizations.

the Bill of Rights	the Vietnam War	the United Nations

Practice 5) Underline the words that have capitalization errors and make the corrections.

1. in august 1959, hawaii became the fiftieth state of the united states.

2. maria is a student from peru. she speaks spanish, french, and english.

3. there are no classes during christmas, easter, and thanksgiving vacations.

4. i have been to the white house in Washington, d.c.

5. students who are buddhist, muslim, christian, and jewish all got together to help.

Unit in a Nutshell

● A comma is used
- To separate items.
- To separate an introductory word/phrase.
- After a dependent clause when it comes first in the sentence.
- To separate two main clauses before a coordinating conjunction (FANBOYS).
- To separate an appositive from the rest of the sentence.

● A colon is used
- To introduce a list of items. This can be useful when writing thesis statements because they allow the writer to introduce the main ideas.

● A semicolon is used
- Between two independent clauses.
- When two independent clauses are joined by a conjunctive adverb: *however, in addition, therefore.*

● An apostrophe is used
- To show possession.
- To indicate a contraction.

Writing in Action

Task 1.

Based on basic punctuation rules you have learned in this unit, edit the following email. Change or add appropriate punctuation.

Dear William

How have you been. I cant believe that the new semester has already started?

I am taking the Practical Reading and Writing course which is required for all sophomore students at Soongsil University. As you know I am not good at English writing however I will try my best to get a good grade.

I have recently started my part-time job at Starbucks. Working during the morning and attending classes are not easy yet I love keeping myself busy.

I am planning to visit you this summer. I already get excited when I think about all the activities that we can do together.

I hope to hear from you soon. Keep in touch.

Best regards
Sung-min

Task 2.

Read the following paragraph. Circle the capitalization errors and make corrections above the errors.

A visit to Cuba

according to an article in last week's issue of newsweek, the prime minister of canada will visit cuba soon in order to establish better economic ties between the two countries. because the united states does not have good relations with cuba, canada's recent decision may result in problems between washington and ottawa. in a recent interviews, peter sheffied, the canadian prime minister, indicated that his country was ready to reestablish some sort of cooperation with cuba and that canada would do so as quickly as possible. There is no doubt that this new development will be discussed at the opening session of congress next tuesday.

Unit 10 Answer Key

Test yourself! (p. 177)

(1) People worship different animals, such as the bird, the dog, and the cow.

(2) William is confident, and he will live a successful life.

(3) I am not tired; therefore, I can do more work.

(4) We have fun by playing games, dancing, and singing.

(5) St. Mary's College is located in Boston, Massachusetts.

(6) My friend and I are taking English 101 class every Thursday.

(7) Americans celebrate Thanksgiving in November.

Practice 1) (p. 182)

1. Nepal is between India and China. (No change)
2. They put garlands around their neck, give them special food, and make them gifts.
3. James bought an expensive car. Therefore, he had to get a car alarm.
4. Before they have the special party, they have a church ceremony.
5. My sister likes doing outdoor activities, while I like reading books at home.
6. The tsunami hit Telewatta, Sri Lanka.
7. Crescent City, California is on the coast.
8. I love to wear sneakers, which are comfortable.
9. The bus which I took this morning broke in the middle of the highway. (Delete the commas)
10. We are going to move out because the living conditions are dangerous. (Delete the comma)

Practice 2) (p. 184)

1. Police kept people away from the scene of the accident; meanwhile, ambulance workers tried to pull victims out of the wreck.
2. Grace works for a prestigious law firm; she is their top criminal lawyer.
3. The future of our wild animals is uncertain; for example, illegal shooting and chemical poisoning threaten many birds.
4. Homework is boring; therefore, I never do it.
5. John studies hard; however, he is not getting good grades.
6. He thinks 8:00 AM is an unreasonable time for class; in contrast, I think it is fine.

Practice 3) (p. 186)

1. Dear Dr. Patterson:
2. To check a book out of the library, you should follow this procedure: write down the call number of the book, find the book, take it to the circulation desk, fill out the card, and show your student I.D.
3. Martin Luther King, Jr., who was an American activist and well-known leader in the Civil Rights Movement, said in his famous speech: I have a dream that my four little children will one day live in a nation where they will not be judged by the color of their skin, but by the content of their character.

Practice 4) (p. 188)

1. Nathan doesn't like to play basketball.
2. The current economic turmoil is everyone's concern.
3. Each office has its own espresso machine.

4. I like Daniel's guitar and his drum.
5. It's raining outside today.

Practice 5) (p. 191)

1. In August 1959, Hawaii became the fiftieth state of the United States.
2. Maria is a student from Peru. She speaks Spanish, French, and English.
3. There are no classes during Christmas, Easter, and Thanksgiving vacations.
4. I have been to the White House in Washington, D.C.
5. Students who are Buddhist, Muslim, Christian, and Jewish all got together to help.

Task 1. (p. 193)

Dear William,

How have you been? I can't believe that the new semester has already started.

I am taking the Practical Reading and Writing course, which is required for all sophomore students at Soongsil University. As you know, I am not good at English writing; however, I will try my best to get a good grade.

I have recently started my part-time job at Starbucks. Working during the morning and attending classes are not easy, yet I love keeping myself busy.

I am planning to visit you this summer. I already get excited when I think about all the activities that we can do together.

I hope to hear from you soon. Keep in touch.

Best regards,
Sung-min

Task 2. (p. 194)

A Visit to Cuba

According to an article in last week's issue of Newsweek, the prime minister of Canada will visit Cuba soon in order to establish better economic ties between the two countries. Because the United States does not have good relations with Cuba, Canada's recent decision may result in problems between Washington and Ottawa. In a recent interview, Peter Sheffield, the Canadian prime minister, indicated that his country was ready to reestablish some sort of cooperation with Cuba and that Canada would do so as quickly as possible. There is no doubt that this new development will be discussed at the opening session of congress next Tuesday.

저자 학력 및 약력 (가나다 순)

| 김형주

한국외대 TESOL 박사수료
현 숭실대 Baird 학부 대학 강사

| 김혜란

University of Massachusetts Amherst TESOL 석사
현 숭실대 Baird 학부 대학 강사

| 백지숙

University of Illinois at Urbana-Champaign 교육학 박사
현 숭실대 Baird 학부대학 전임 교수

| 송은혜

University of Leeds 영어교육학 박사
현 숭실대 Baird 학부대학 전임 교수

| Elizabeth Houtrow

Duke University 경영학 석사
현 숭실대 Baird 학부대학 전임 교수

Grammar for
Writing in English

초판발행 2011년 3월 7일
2쇄발행 2013년 11월 10일

| 지은이 _ 김형주, 김혜란, 백지숙,
송은혜, Elizabeth Houtrow
| 펴낸이 _ 한헌수
| 펴낸곳 _ 숭실대학교출판국
서울시 동작구 상도로 369
| 등 록 _ 제14-2호(1982. 1. 25)
TEL. 02-820-0771~2
FAX. 02-817-5297
http://press.ssu.ac.kr
| 찍은곳 _ 한컴인쇄정보
TEL. 02-2274-3394
FAX. 02-2274-3397

[값 13,000원]

ISBN 978-89-7450-265-2 03740